Student Workbook

AGS
PUBLISHING

Algebra

AGS Publishing
Circle Pines, MN 55014-1796
800-328-2560

© 2004 AGS Publishing
4201 Woodland Road
Circle Pines, MN 55014-1796
800-328-2560 • www.agsnet.com

AGS Publishing is a trademark and trade name of American Guidance Service, Inc.

Printed in the United States of America

ISBN 0-7854-3569-7

Product Number 93823

19 20

Table of Contents

Arithmetic and Algebra

EXAMPLE	$16 + 2 = 22$	*false*
	$10 \div 5 = 2$	*true*
	$33 - n = 12$	*open*

Directions Write *true* if the statement is true or *false* if it is false. Write *open* if the statement is neither true nor false.

1. $11 + 5 = 16$ _____

2. $11 + 3 = 16$ _____

3. $7 - 7 = 0$ _____

4. $6 \cdot 6 = 36$ _____

5. $12 + n = 17$ _____

6. $32 \div 8 = 4$ _____

7. $2 \cdot 3 = 5$ _____

8. $\frac{22}{11} = 3$ _____

9. $100 + 10 = 120$ _____

10. $7n = 49$ _____

11. $7 \cdot 7 = 49$ _____

12. $37 - n = 12$ _____

13. $\frac{n}{2} = 6$ _____

14. $60 - 60 = 10$ _____

15. $17 \cdot 1 = 18$ _____

16. $50 - 5 = 45$ _____

17. $\frac{18}{3} = 6$ _____

18. $30 + 30 = 60$ _____

19. $22n = 44$ _____

20. $27 \div 9 = 3$ _____

21. $27 - 9 = 18$ _____

22. $6 \cdot 6 = 38$ _____

23. $11 + n = 35$ _____

24. $15 \div 3 = 4$ _____

25. $18 \div 9 = 2$ _____

26. $8n = 112$ _____

27. $4 \cdot 4 = 8$ _____

28. $14 - n = 1$ _____

29. $\frac{6}{2} = 3$ _____

30. $7 + 27 = 35$ _____

Representing Numbers Using Letters

EXAMPLE

Numerical expressions:	$33 - 13$	$\frac{36}{12}$
Algebraic expressions:	$2m \div 5$	$8d + 2$
Variables:	n in $7n + 7$	k in $k - 3$
Operations:	Multiplication and addition in $2y + 3$	Division in $\frac{14}{2}$

Directions Name the variable in each algebraic expression.

1. $4y + 12$ _____

2. $k - 6$ _____

3. $2x + 7$ _____

4. $7n$ _____

5. $\frac{2m}{4}$ _____

6. $3(d)$ _____

7. $\frac{r}{4}$ _____

8. $14k - 10$ _____

9. $x - 100$ _____

10. $3 \div p$ _____

11. $4 + y$ _____

12. $2m \div 5$ _____

Directions Fill in the table. For each expression, write the expression type—*numerical* or *algebraic*—and list the operation or operations.

Expression	Expression Type	Operation(s)
$16 \div 2$	**13.**	**14.**
$8d$	**15.**	**16.**
$5 + 11$	**17.**	**18.**
$\frac{36}{12}$	**19.**	**20.**
$2p - 1$	**21.**	**22.**
$4k + 4$	**23.**	**24.**

Directions Solve the problem.

25. Only 17 members of Mr. Ricardo's class are going on the class trip.
The class has a total of k students. Write an algebraic expression
for the number of students who are *not* going on the trip. _____

Integers on the Number Line

EXAMPLE

-8 -7 -6 -5 -4 -3 -2 -1 0 1 2 3 4 5 6 7 8

- All the numbers on this number line are examples of *integers.*
- An example of a *negative integer* is –5 (see arrow).
- An example of a *positive integer* is 5 (see arrow).
- The number 0 is neither negative nor positive.
- |–5| = 5. In other words, –5 is 5 units from 0 (count the units).
- |5| = 5. In other words, 5 is 5 units from 0 (count the units).

Directions Identify each integer as either *negative, positive,* or *zero.*

1. 6 _____

2. 13 _____

3. –2 _____

4. 11 _____

5. 8 _____

6. –9 _____

7. 0 _____

8. –33 _____

9. 20 _____

10. 1 _____

11. 7 _____

12. –1 _____

Directions Write each absolute value.

13. |–5| _____

14. |6| _____

15. |–2| _____

16. |2| _____

17. |+18| _____

18. |5| _____

19. |–11| _____

20. |–12| _____

21. |12| _____

22. |4| _____

23. |–9| _____

24. |9| _____

Directions Solve this problem.

25. On the number line, how could you represent $5 that you earned?
How could you represent $5 that you had to pay? _____

Adding Integers

EXAMPLE   Add 2 + (–5).

Start at 2, move 5 units to the *left*. The answer is –3.

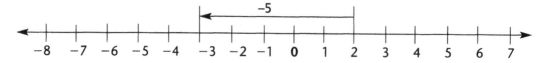

Add –3 + 7.

Start at –3, move 7 units to the *right*. The answer is 4.

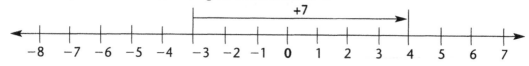

Directions   Answer the questions.

1. To add a *negative* number, in which direction do you count on the number line? _____

2. To add a *positive* number, in which direction do you count on the number line? _____

Directions   Write each sum on the blank.

3. –4 + 4 _____	**12.** –2 + (–4) _____
4. 1 + (–7) _____	**13.** –6 + 6 _____
5. 1 + 5 _____	**14.** 6 + (–6) _____
6. 0 + 6 _____	**15.** –4 + 8 _____
7. –1 + (–5) _____	**16.** –6 + 12 _____
8. 5 + (–11) _____	**17.** –2 + 6 _____
9. –5 + 3 _____	**18.** –3 + 9 _____
10. –6 + 3 _____	**19.** 7 + 7 _____
11. 11 + (–12) _____	**20.** 2 + (–8) _____

Subtracting Integers

EXAMPLE   Find the difference: 14 − (−15)

Rule   To subtract in algebra, add the opposite.

15 is the opposite of −15.

14 + 15 = 29

Directions Rewrite each expression as addition. Solve the new
expression.

1. −4 − (−11) _____

2. 9 − (+3) _____

3. −1 − 13 _____

4. −6 − (+10) _____

5. 7 − (−10) _____

6. 4 − (+4) _____

7. 2 − (+8) _____

8. −11 − (−1) _____

9. 6 − (+2) _____

10. −5 − (−5) _____

11. 2 − (+9) _____

12. 1 − (+4) _____

13. 6 − 8 _____

14. −8 − (−3) _____

15. −3 − (+7) _____

16. 8 − (−7) _____

17. 10 − (+5) _____

18. 5 − 6 _____

Directions Solve these problems. Write an expression and the answer.

19. Dara's kite is flying 67 feet high. Jill's is flying
40 feet high. What is the difference between
the heights of these two kites?

_____

20. A helicopter hovers 60 m above the ocean's
surface. A submarine is resting 30 m
underwater, directly below the helicopter.
What is the difference between the positions of
these two objects?

_____

Multiplying Integers

EXAMPLE   Notice the possible combinations for multiplying positive and negative integers.

     positive (positive) = positive $4(4)$ $= 16$

     positive (negative) = negative $4(-4)$ $= -16$

     negative (positive) = negative $-4(4)$ $= -16$

     negative (negative) = positive $-4(-4)$ $= 16$

     Multiplying any integer, positive or negative, by 0 gives 0 as the product.

Directions Tell whether the product is *positive*, *negative*, or *zero*.

1. $(4)(-7)$ _____

2. $(-6)(3)$ _____

3. $(-7)(0)$ _____

4. $(-9)(-9)$ _____

5. $(2)(-11)$ _____

6. $(5)(-3)$ _____

7. $(-15)(-1)$ _____

8. $(0)(14)$ _____

9. $(-5)(7)$ _____

10. $(-8)(-2)$ _____

11. $(-3)(-9)$ _____

12. $(4)(6)$ _____

13. $(11)(-2)$ _____

14. $(2)(9)$ _____

15. $(-6)(4)$ _____

Directions Find each product. Write the answer.

16. $(2)(9)$ _____

17. $(-5)(9)$ _____

18. $(3)(-9)$ _____

19. $(-10)(2)$ _____

20. $(-9)(-7)$ _____

21. $(-5)(10)$ _____

22. $(12)(2)$ _____

23. $(-32)(0)$ _____

24. $(6)(-4)$ _____

25. $(-11)(-2)$ _____

26. $(-4)(8)$ _____

27. $(-10)(-8)$ _____

28. $(5)(-5)$ _____

29. $(-1)(-1)$ _____

30. $(7)(10)$ _____

Integers

Data from a climbing expedition is shown in this table.

Elevation in Feet (Compared to Sea Level)	
Base Camp	−384
Camp 1	+5,027
Camp 2	+7,511
Camp 3	+8,860
Camp 4	+10,103
Camp 5	+10,856
Camp 6	+11,349
Summit	+12,015

During the climb, some climbers began at base camp and climbed to the summit. Other climbers also began at base camp but did not reach the summit—these climbers moved back and forth between camps carrying supplies and other necessities.

Directions The movements of various climbers in the expedition are shown below. Find the number of feet climbed by each climber.

1. Climber A: Base Camp to Camp 1 to Base Camp _____

2. Climber C: Base Camp to Camp 5 to Base Camp _____

3. Climber F: Base Camp to Camp 3 to Base Camp _____

4. Climber B: Base Camp to Camp 2 to Base Camp _____

5. Climber H: Base Camp to Camp 6 to Base Camp _____

6. Climber E: Base Camp to Summit to Base Camp _____

7. Climber G: Base Camp to Camp 4 to Base Camp _____

8. Climber D: Base Camp to Camp 5 to Camp 3
to Camp 4 to Base Camp _____

9. Climber I: Base Camp to Camp 2 to Camp 1
to Camp 6 to Base Camp _____

10. How many feet above base camp is the summit? _____

Dividing Positive and Negative Integers

EXAMPLE Notice the possible combinations for dividing positive and negative integers.

positive ÷ positive = positive	$6 \div 2$	$= 3$
positive ÷ negative = negative	$6 \div -2$	$= -3$
negative ÷ positive = negative	$-6 \div 2$	$= -3$
negative ÷ negative = positive	$-6 \div -2$	$= 3$

Dividing 0 by any integer, positive or negative, produces 0 as the quotient.

Directions Tell whether the quotient is *positive*, *negative*, or *zero*.

1. $16 \div -4$ _____

2. $-63 \div -9$ _____

3. $-10 \div 2$ _____

4. $33 \div 11$ _____

5. $-12 \div 4$ _____

6. $100 \div 10$ _____

7. $36 \div -9$ _____

8. $15 \div -5$ _____

9. $-27 \div 3$ _____

10. $0 \div -4$ _____

11. $-81 \div -9$ _____

12. $19 \div -1$ _____

13. $56 \div 8$ _____

14. $500 \div 5$ _____

15. $32 \div -8$ _____

Directions Find and write each quotient.

16. $36 \div 12$ _____

17. $21 \div -7$ _____

18. $18 \div -3$ _____

19. $-35 \div 7$ _____

20. $-24 \div 2$ _____

21. $-16 \div -8$ _____

22. $45 \div -9$ _____

23. $-200 \div -200$ _____

24. $-50 \div 10$ _____

25. $27 \div -9$ _____

26. $-14 \div 2$ _____

27. $0 \div 16$ _____

28. $-72 \div -9$ _____

29. $-1 \div -1$ _____

30. $9 \div 3$ _____

Simplifying Expressions—One Variable

EXAMPLE Simplify $2n + 2 + 4n$.

    1. Look for like terms. $2n$ and $4n$ are like terms, because they have the same variable, n.

    2. Combine the terms: $2n + 4n = 6n$

    3. Rewrite the whole expression: $6n + 2$

    Now you are finished, because $6n$ cannot combine with 2.

Directions In each expression, underline the like terms.

1. $3k - 8 + 2k$

2. $p + 12 + p$

3. $100 + 4w + 4w$

4. $5m - 3 + 2m$

5. $7x + 5x - 12$

6. $-2 + 11c + c$

7. $\frac{4}{7} + 2m + 3m$

8. $2y - (-3y) + 7$

9. $4x - 13 + 5x$

10. $8r + (-3r)$

Directions Simplify each expression.

11. $3b + b$ _____

12. $11y + 2y + y$ _____

13. $7j + 3j - 2j$ _____

14. $2k - 17 + k$ _____

15. $11x + x - 14$ _____

16. $22 + 2d + 8d$ _____

17. $9g + (-2g) + 4$ _____

18. $14h - 3 - 2h$ _____

19. $2m + (-8m)$ _____

20. $3 + 4k - 3k$ _____

21. $2y + (-2y) + 5$ _____

22. $-5 + 6n - 4n$ _____

23. $2x + 11x - 13$ _____

24. $-h + 7h$ _____

25. $-11 - (-3k) + k$ _____

26. $7d - d + 40$ _____

27. $8 + 3m - (-m)$ _____

28. $3w + (-5w)$ _____

29. $2 + 5x - 2x$ _____

30. $8g + (-5g) - 6$ _____

Simplifying Expressions—Several Variables

EXAMPLE   Simplify $2j + 4 + j - 1 + 3k$.

   1. Scan for variables. The expression has two: j and k.

   2. Combine j terms: $2j + j = 3j$

   3. Combine k terms: $3k$ (no combining required)

   4. Combine integers: $4 + (-1) = +3$

   5. Rewrite the whole expression: $3j + 3k + 3$

   Now you are finished, because you cannot combine unlike terms.

Directions Check the column or columns to show which kinds of terms
               each expression includes.

Expression	x terms	y terms	Integers
1. $3x + 2x + 3 + 6y$			
2. $3y - 14$			
3. $x + 2y - 10 + 3y$			
4. $72 - 68$			
5. $x - 8$			

Directions Combine like terms. Simplify each expression.

   6. $3k - 2k + 12 + 5r$ _____

   7. $2c + 3b + 8b + c$ _____

   8. $5k + 3 + 2j - 2 - k$ _____

   9. $7 + 4p - 6 + 2m - 2p$ _____

   10. $-4n + 4 - (-2d) + n - 5$ _____

   11. $18 + (-4x) + 1 - 3x + 8y$ _____

   12. $2w + (-11) + 18y + 2w - 11$ _____

   13. $6h - 12 - 9h + 8k + (-3k)$ _____

   14. $3 - 3m - 3m - 8p - 3p$ _____

   15. $14x - 7 + 3y - 7x - 7x$ _____

Positive Exponents

EXAMPLE   To multiply *like* variables having exponents, add the exponents.

$$k^3 \cdot k^3 = k^{(3+3)} = k^6$$

To divide *like* variables having exponents, subtract the exponents.

$$m^4 \div m^2 = m^{(4-2)} = m^2$$

You *cannot* use these rules to multiply or divide unlike variables.

$$y^3 \cdot a^2 \qquad b^5 \div j^2$$

Directions   Is the rewritten expression on the right *true* or *false*? Write the answer.

1. $m^4 \cdot m^2 = m^{(4+2)}$ _____

2. $a \cdot a \cdot a = a^{(1+1+1)}$ _____

3. $k^2 \cdot n^3 = k^{(2+3)}$ _____

4. $y^7 \div y = y^{(7-1)}$ _____

5. $b^8 \div b^3 = b^{(8-3)}$ _____

6. $a \cdot a = 2a$ _____

7. $d^6 \div d^2 = d^{(6+2)}$ _____

8. $w^2 \cdot w^4 \cdot w^5 = w^{(2+4+5)}$ _____

Directions   Simplify each expression.

9. $k^3 \cdot k^3$ _____   **13.** $d^2 \cdot d^5 \cdot d^7$ _____

10. $w^5 \div w^2$ _____   **14.** $y^7 \div y$ _____

11. $j^{14} \div j^{10}$ _____   **15.** $x^2 \cdot x^3 \cdot x^8$ _____

12. $n^6 \cdot n$ _____   **16.** $a^2 \cdot a^2 \cdot a^4 \cdot a^4$ _____

Directions   Use a calculator to find the value of each expression.

17. x^2 when $x = 17$ _____   **19.** r^5 when $r = 3$ _____

18. c^5 when $c = 2$ _____   **20.** k^3 when $k = 0.8$ _____

Formulas with Variables

EXAMPLE Find the perimeter of a triangle with unequal sides.

The perimeter is the *sum* of the length of all the sides.

Perimeter = $a + b + c$

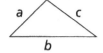

If $a = 3$, $b = 5$, and $c = 4$, then the perimeter of the triangle is $3 + 5 + 4 = 12$.

Directions Use the formula for the perimeter of a triangle with unequal sides to find each answer.

1. $a = 8$ cm

$b = 10$ cm   Perimeter = _____

$c = 6$ cm

2. $a = 2$ m

$b = 7$ m   Perimeter = _____

$c = 3$ m

Directions Use the formula for the perimeter of a square. Write each answer.

3. $s = 5$ km

Perimeter = _____

Perimeter of a square = $4s$

4. $s = 18$ cm

Perimeter = _____

5. $s = 9$ m

Perimeter = _____

Commutative Property of Addition

EXAMPLE $2n + 3n =$ _____

Expanded notation:

$n + n$ $+$ $n + n + n$ $=$ $n + n + n + n + n$

$2n$ $+$ $3n$ $=$ $5n$

Commutative property of addition:

$7a + 6a = 6a + 7a$

Directions Find each sum using expanded notation.

1. $k + 3k$ _____

2. $2r + r$ _____

3. $4y + y$ _____

4. $n + 5n$ _____

Directions Rewrite each sum showing the commutative property of addition.

5. $b + 17$ _____

9. $5m + 3p$ _____

6. $3k + 5$ _____

10. $7q + 6$ _____

7. $x + 5x$ _____

11. $164 + 133$ _____

8. $2.7 + 1.2$ _____

12. $8y + 4y$ _____

Directions Solve these problems.

13. Torri weighs 98 pounds. Carrie weighs 116 pounds. Torri adds her weight to Carrie's weight.

What sum will she get? _____

14. Suppose Carrie adds her weight to Torri's weight. What sum will she get? _____

15. What mathematical property do the sums in problems 13 and 14 illustrate?

_____

Commutative Property of Multiplication

EXAMPLE | Turning a rectangle two different ways shows that the order of factors in a product can change without affecting the result. In each case, the product is the area of the rectangle in square units.

Factors	Product	
5 • 3 =	15	5 [rectangle] 3

Factors	Product	
3 • 5 =	15	3 [rectangle] 5

Directions For each pair of rectangles, write two products representing area in square units.

1.

1 [rectangle] 7

7 [rectangle] 1

_____ • _____ = _____ sq. units   _____ • _____ = _____ sq. units

2.

3 [rectangle] 6

6 [rectangle] 3

_____ • _____ = _____ sq. units   _____ • _____ = _____ sq. units

Directions Answer the questions.

Mrs. Rossi buys 6 bags of apples. Each bag holds 8 apples. Mr. Lundgren buys 8 bags of apples. Each bag holds 6 apples.

3. How many apples did Mrs. Rossi buy? _____

4. How many apples did Mr. Lundgren buy? _____

5. What mathematical property do problems 3 and 4 illustrate?

_____

Associative Property of Addition

EXAMPLE

$(13 + 10) + 4 = 13 + (10 + 4)$

$(b + c) + d = b + (c + d)$

Directions Rewrite each expression to show the associative property of addition.

1. $3k + (2k + 5)$ _____

4. $7 + (5 + q)$ _____

2. $(1.3 + 8.1) + 6.6$ _____

5. $(3 + 12n) + 2$ _____

3. $(11x + 10y) + 4$ _____

6. $g + (21 + h)$ _____

Directions Answer the questions.

In a club, 3 members bring all of the sandwiches for a picnic.

- Mike and Lynn arrive together. They have already put together Mike's 3 sandwiches and Lynn's 5 sandwiches.

- Hosea comes a little later with 4 sandwiches. In all, the club has a total of 12 sandwiches.

7. Write an addition expression that shows the grouping described above.

_____

8. Suppose that Mike had come first, alone, and that Lynn and Hosea had come with their combined sandwiches later. Write an addition expression to represent this grouping.

_____

9. Would the club's total number of sandwiches be the same with either grouping?

_____

10. What mathematical property does this story illustrate?

_____ _____

Associative Property of Multiplication

EXAMPLE $(5 \cdot 2)3$ $=$ $5(2 \cdot 3)$

$(pq)r$ $=$ $p(qr)$

Directions   Use the associative property of multiplication to place
parentheses in two different ways.

1. mnq _____ _____

2. abc _____ _____

3. $4st$ _____ _____

4. kvz _____ _____

5. $1.5bc$ _____ _____

6. $9mn$ _____ _____

7. aks _____ _____

Directions   Answer the questions to solve the problem.

A college will build a theater with at least 30 balcony seats. Two architects
have drawn up plans. Here are their designs for the balconies:

Plan A: **6 Seats**

3 rows

Plan B: **6 Seats**

2 rows

8. Which plan does $(3 \cdot 6)2$ describe? _____
Hint: Think of the parentheses as "inside" dimensions.

9. Which plan does $3(6 \cdot 2)$ describe? _____

10. Do the two plans have the same number of balcony seats? _____

The Distributive Property—Multiplication

EXAMPLE $4(2 + 8) = 4 \cdot 2 + 4 \cdot 8 = 8 + 32 = 40$

$5(x + y) = 5 \cdot x + 5 \cdot y = 5x + 5y$

Directions Fill in the blanks in each rewritten expression.

1. $2(x + y) = 2x + \underline{\quad}y$

2. $4(m + 4) = 4\underline{\quad} + 16$

3. $7(8 + 1) = 56 + \underline{\quad}$

4. $5(4 + c) = 20 + \underline{\quad}$

5. $-1(p + q) = \underline{\quad} - q$

6. $8(a + 1) = 8a + \underline{\quad}$

7. $-2(-j + k) = \underline{\quad} - 2k$

8. $-10(40 + 30) = -400 - \underline{\quad}$

9. $2[-q + (-3)] = \underline{\quad} - 6$

10. $-4(-3 + n) = \underline{\quad} - 4n$

11. $3(-7 + b) = -21 + \underline{\quad}$

12. $7(d + 2k) = 7d + \underline{\quad}$

13. $-4(5 + 1) = \underline{\quad} - 4$

14. $-11(n + p) = \underline{\quad} - 11p$

15. $k(13 + m) = 13k + \underline{\quad}$

16. $b(y + z) = \underline{\quad} + bz$

Directions Rewrite each expression, using the distributive property. Simplify where possible.

17. $16(2 + 1)$ _____

18. $6(r + z)$ _____

19. $-1(d + k)$ _____

20. $3(11 + w)$ _____

21. $-2(-4 + m)$ _____

22. $8[-a + (-3)]$ _____

23. $-9(x + y)$ _____

24. $7(g + 10)$ _____

25. $-8(-v + 8)$ _____

The Distributive Property—Factoring

EXAMPLE

$4j + 4k = 4(j + k)$

$3x^2 - 3y^2 = 3(x^2 - y^2)$

Directions   Identify the common factor in each expression.

1. $11k + 11w$ _____

2. $jn + kn$ _____

3. $-2q + (-2r)$ _____

4. $12b - 13b$ _____

5. $3p + 46p$ _____

6. $dx^3 - dy^2$ _____

7. $1.9a + 1.9b$ _____

8. $3r - 1.5r$ _____

9. $7m^2 + 7v^2$ _____

Directions   Draw a line to match the expression on the left with its factored form on the right.

10. $7x - 7y$

11. $ax + ay$

12. $4x + 4y$

13. $-2x + 2y$

14. $3ax + 3y$

a. $a(x + y)$

b. $-2(x - y)$

c. $3(ax + y)$

d. $7(x - y)$

e. $4(x + y)$

Directions   Solve the problem.

15. Two children are paid their allowances in dimes and nickels. Each child receives exactly the same number of each type of coin.

Let d stand for the number of dimes each child received. Let n stand for the number of nickels each received. One way to represent total amount of allowance to the children is $2d + 2n$. What is another way? (Hint: Use the distributive property to factor.)

_____

Properties of Zero

EXAMPLE

Additive Property of Zero:	$4 + 0 = 4$	$-2 + 0 = -2$
Additive Inverse Property:	$-3 + 3 = 0$	$5 + (-5) = 0$
Multiplication Property of Zero:	$0(6) = 0$	$-4(0) = 0$

Directions If the two numbers are additive inverses, write *true*.
Otherwise, write *false*.

1. -12 12 _____

2. 7 -7 _____

3. -5 0 _____

4. -75 75 _____

5. -8 -8 _____

6. x $-x$ _____

Directions Write each sum.

7. $9 + 0$ _____

8. $0 + 27$ _____

9. $0 - 14$ _____

10. $k + 0$ _____

11. $-16 + 0$ _____

12. $0 + m^2$ _____

13. $0 - 37$ _____

14. $k^5 + 0$ _____

15. $0 - y^2$ _____

Directions Write each product.

16. $0(112)$ _____

17. $(-17)(0)$ _____

18. $0 \cdot q$ _____

19. $(xy)(0)$ _____

20. $(0)(-9)$ _____

21. $(cde)(0)$ _____

22. $(-jk)(0)$ _____

23. $n^7 \cdot 0$ _____

24. $(0)(ab^3)$ _____

Directions Solve the problem.

25. Jenna said to Brett, "I'll give you double the number of marbles you have in your pocket."
Brett replied, "But I don't have *any* marbles in my pocket."
Jenna responded, "So I'll give you double nothing, which is nothing."

How could Jenna say the same thing in a mathematical expression? Underline one.

    a. $1 + 2 = 3$ **b.** $0 + 2 = 2$ **c.** $2(0) = 0$

Properties of 1

EXAMPLE   Multiplication Property of 1: $(1)(7) = 7$ $(1)(y) = y$

Multiplicative Reciprocals: $\frac{1}{8}$, 8: $\frac{1}{8} \cdot \frac{8}{1} = 1$ $\frac{1}{x}$, x: $\frac{1}{x} \cdot \frac{x}{1} = 1$

Directions Complete the table by writing the reciprocal of the term and then checking your answer.

	Term	Reciprocal	Check
1.	$\frac{1}{4}$	_____	_____
2.	$\frac{1}{9}$	_____	_____
3.	7	_____	_____
4.	$\frac{1}{12}$	_____	_____
5.	k	_____	_____
6.	$\frac{1}{m}$	_____	_____
7.	c^2	_____	_____
8.	3	_____	_____

Directions Solve the problems.

9. Each wedge of apple pie is $\frac{1}{5}$ of the pie. How many wedges make one whole pie? Complete the equation to show your answer.

$\frac{1}{5} \cdot$ _____ $= 1$

10. In a geometry study group, 6 students were each given an identical puzzle piece of a hexagon (6-sided figure). The students assembled their pieces to make a whole hexagon. What fraction of the hexagon was each puzzle piece? Complete the equation to show your answer.

$6 \cdot$ _____ $= 1$

Powers and Roots

EXAMPLE	$3^2 = (3)(3) = 9$	$\sqrt{9} = 3$
	$3^3 = (3)(3)(3) = 27$	$\sqrt[3]{27} = 3$

Directions Fill in the blank in each sentence.

1. $(19)(19)(19) = 6{,}859$, so _____$^3 = 6{,}859$.

2. If $17 \cdot 17 = 289$, then $17^2 = 289$ and $\sqrt{289} =$ _____.

3. If $\sqrt[3]{216} = 6$, then 6 _____ $= 216$.

4. If $2 \cdot 2 \cdot 2 \cdot 2 = 16$, then the fourth _____ of 16 is 2.

5. $(4)(4)(4)(4)(4) = 1{,}024$, so 4 _____ $= 1{,}024$.

6. $11^2 = 121$, which means that $11 \cdot$ _____ $= 121$.

Directions Find each square root. You may use a calculator.

7. $\sqrt{49}$ _____

8. $\sqrt{81}$ _____

9. $\sqrt{16}$ _____

10. $\sqrt{225}$ _____

11. $\sqrt{729}$ _____

12. $\sqrt{4}$ _____

13. $\sqrt{5{,}929}$ _____

14. $\sqrt{3.61}$ _____

15. $\sqrt{10.24}$ _____

16. $\sqrt{100}$ _____

17. $\sqrt{182.25}$ _____

18. $\sqrt{36}$ _____

Directions Solve the problems.

19. Talia is sewing a quilt with a regular checkerboard pattern—that is, all the squares are identical. In each square of the checkerboard, she plans to stitch a simple flower. Talia will have to stitch 36 flowers in all. How many squares lie along one side of the quilt?

_____

20. The volume of a cube of sugar is 2.197 cm^3. Circle the letter of the expression that gives the length of one edge of the cube.

a. $\sqrt[3]{2.197}$ b. $(1.3)^3$ c. $\sqrt{2.197}$

More on Powers and Roots

EXAMPLE Simplify the expression: $(-2x)^3$

    Step 1 $(-2x)^3 = (-2x)(-2x)(-2x)$

    Step 2   Multiply (-2) three times: $(-2)(-2)(-2)$ = -8

    Step 3   Multiply x three times: $(x)(x)(x)$ = x^3

    Step 4   Multiply the expanded number and variable: $-8x^3$

    Note: $\sqrt{x^2} = x$ or $-x$ $\sqrt[3]{x^3} = x$ $\sqrt[3]{-x^3} = -x$

Directions   Simplify each term. You can use a calculator.

1. $(8d)^2$ _____

2. $(-10n)^2$ _____

3. $(-2y)^3$ _____

4. $(3m)^4$ _____

Directions   Find each value. Write all the possible roots.

5. $\sqrt{16}$ _____   **8.** $\sqrt[3]{-8}$ _____   **11.** $\sqrt[3]{-27}$ _____

6. $\sqrt{9}$ _____   **9.** $\sqrt{k^2}$ _____   **12.** $\sqrt[3]{-216}$ _____

7. $\sqrt[3]{8}$ _____   **10.** $\sqrt{100}$ _____   **13.** $\sqrt[3]{216}$ _____

Directions   Answer the questions to solve the problem.

If a scientist built a machine that could transport people backward in time, then normal time might be represented as a positive number and backward time as a negative number. Suppose you could square or cube backward time.

14. What would be the square of -10 units of backward time?   _____

15. What would be the cube of -10 units of backward time?   _____

Order of Operations

EXAMPLE	$2^3 + 12 \cdot 8 =$

Step 1 Calculate the cube, or third power, of 2: $2^3 = 8$

Step 2 Multiply: $12 \cdot 8 = 96$

Step 3 Add: $8 + 96 = 104$

Directions Find the value using the order of operations.

1. $11 - 2 \cdot 3$ _____

2. $2 + 8 \cdot 7$ _____

3. $(2 + 8)7$ _____

4. $64 - 16 \cdot 4$ _____

5. $2 + 2^3$ _____

6. $3 + 27 \div 9$ _____

7. $18 \div 2 + 100$ _____

8. $2 + 5^2 \cdot 4$ _____

9. $2^2 + 3^2 + 2^4$ _____

10. $(7 \cdot 7 - 4) \div 15$ _____

11. $(6 + 6) \div (59 - 55)$ _____

12. $8^2 - 7^2$ _____

Directions Answer the questions to solve the problem.

Mr. and Mrs. Wang plan to knock out a wall between two rooms of their house to make one larger room. One room is a rectangle 10 feet by 15 feet, so its area in square feet is 10(15). The other room is a square, 9 feet on a side, so its area is 9^2 square feet. What will be the total area of the new room?

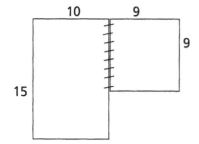

13. Circle the letter of the expression that calculates the answer.

   a. $10 + 15 \cdot 9^2$ **b.** $(10 + 15 + 9)^2$ **c.** $10 \cdot 15 + 9^2$

14. State the order to perform the operations when calculating the answer.

   (1) _____   **(2)** _____   **(3)** _____

15. Work out the answer. (You can use a calculator.) _____ square feet

Order of Operations

EXAMPLE

The answer shown below for the computation $10 + 6 \div 2$ is not correct.

$10 + 6 \div 2$
$\downarrow$
$16 \div 2$
$\downarrow$
8

The computation is not correct because the addition $10 + 6$ was performed first.
The order of operations states that the division $6 \div 2$ should have been performed first.

The answer is 13 when the computation is performed correctly.

$10 + 6 \div 2$
$\downarrow$
$10 + 3$
$\downarrow$
13

Directions In each problem below, the computation has been performed incorrectly. For each problem, tell why the computation is incorrect. Then give the correct answer.

1. $2 + 4 \cdot 5 = 30$ _____

2. $20 \div 5 + 5 = 2$ _____

3. $50 \cdot 2 - 2 = 0$ _____

4. $24 + 6 \div 3 = 10$ _____

5. $100 \div 50 \cdot 2 = 1$ _____

6. $5 \cdot 8 + 1 = 45$ _____

7. $200 - 100 + 50 \div 2 = 75$ _____

8. $42 \div 6 \cdot 7 = 1$ _____

9. $2 + 16 \div 4 + 4 = 4$ _____

10. $10 \cdot 4 \div 2 + 1 = 30$ _____

Writing Equations

EXAMPLE	10 times some number equals 30.
	$10x = 30$

Directions Write an equation for each statement. Let x be the variable in the equation.

1. 6 times some number equals 30. _____

2. 2 times some number plus 5 equals 9. _____

3. 3 times some number minus 8 equals 1. _____

4. 17 subtracted from some number equals 14. _____

5. 10 times some number plus 7 equals 87. _____

6. 11 subtracted from some number equals 2. _____

EXAMPLE	$3x = 18$	$x = 4, 5, 6$
	$(3)(4) = 18$	F
	$(3)(5) = 18$	F
	$(3)(6) = 18$	T

Directions Find the root of each equation by performing the operation on each value for the variable. Write T if the equation is true or F if the equation is false.

7. $5p = 15$

$p = 1$ _____

$p = 2$ _____

$p = 3$ _____

8. $7w = 49$

$w = 5$ _____

$w = 6$ _____

$w = 7$ _____

9. $10k = 80$

$k = 7$ _____

$k = 8$ _____

$k = 9$ _____

10. $2a = 22$

$a = 11$ _____

$a = 12$ _____

$a = 13$ _____

Solving Equations: $x - b = c$

EXAMPLE   Solve $m - 2 = 8$ for m.

Step 1	Write the equation.	$m - 2 = 8$
Step 2	Add 2 to both sides of the equation.	$m - 2 + 2 = 8 + 2$
Step 3	Simplify.	$m = 10$
Step 4	Check.	$10 - 2 = 8$

Directions Solve each equation. Check your answer.

1. $x - 4 = 20$ _____

2. $b - 7 = 1$ _____

3. $n - 2 = 7$ _____

4. $k - 13 = 3$ _____

5. $d - 100 = 100$ _____

6. $c - 11 = 0$ _____

7. $y - 4 = 14$ _____

8. $r - 80 = 20$ _____

9. $w - 8 = 0$ _____

Directions Read the problem and follow the directions.

10. A sports store buys a shipment of catcher's mitts at the beginning of
the year. By year's end, the store has sold 100 mitts and has 150 left.
How many mitts did the store have at the first of the year?

Let x stand for the number of catcher's mitts the store had at the
beginning of the year: $x - 100 = 150$

How would you solve this equation? Circle the answer.

   a. Subtract 100 from both sides.

   b. Add 100 to both sides.

   c. Subtract 150 from both sides.

Solving Equations: $x + b = c$

EXAMPLE	Solve $k + 5 = 9$ for k.	
	Step 1 Write the equation.	$k + 5 = 9$
	Step 2 Subtract 5 from both sides of the equation.	$k + 5 - 5 = 9 - 5$
	Step 3 Simplify.	$k = 4$
	Step 4 Check.	$4 + 5 = 9$

Directions Solve each equation. Check your answer.

1. $w + 3 = 4$ _____

2. $r + 8 = 12$ _____

3. $y + 2 = 7$ _____

4. $c + 1.5 = 4.5$ _____

5. $k + 22 = 60$ _____

6. $d + 9 = 18$ _____

7. $n + 5 = 40$ _____

8. $b + 7 = 14$ _____

9. $x + 32 = 38$ _____

Directions Read the problem and follow the directions.

10. Amy read 17 books over the summer, 11 more than Tim. How many books did Tim read?

Let r stand for the number of books Tim read over the summer:
$$r + 11 = 17$$

How would you solve this equation? Circle the answer.

a. Add 11 to both sides.

b. Subtract 11 from both sides.

c. Subtract 17 from both sides.

Solving Multiplication Equations

EXAMPLE Solve $4y = 16$ for y.

    Step 1 Write the equation. $4y = 16$

    Step 2 Multiply both sides of the equation
               by $\frac{1}{4}$, the reciprocal of 4. $(\frac{1}{4})4y = 16(\frac{1}{4})$

    Step 3 Simplify. $y = 4$

    Step 4 Check. $4 \bullet 4 = 16$

    Note: Another way to do Step 2 is to *divide*
               both sides of the equation by 4. $\frac{4y}{4} = \frac{16}{4}$

Directions Solve each equation. Check your answer.

1. $2q = 14$ _____

2. $10k = 30$ _____

3. $7x = 28$ _____

4. $3d = 18$ _____

5. $6w = 66$ _____

6. $4j = -16$ _____

7. $8y = 48$ _____

8. $-5n = -20$ _____

9. $3.2p = 12.8$ _____

Directions Read the problem and follow the directions.

10. Juanita is 15, five times the age of her brother, Frank. How old is Frank?

Let a stand for Frank's age: $5a = 15$

How would you solve this equation? Circle the answer.

  a. Subtract 5 from both sides of the equation.

  b. Multiply both sides of the equation by 5.

  c. Multiply both sides of the equation by $\frac{1}{5}$.

Solving Equations with Fractions

EXAMPLE   Solve $\frac{1}{3}y = 5$ for y.

Step 1	Write the equation.	$\frac{1}{3}y = 5$
Step 2	Multiply both sides of the equation by the reciprocal of the fraction.	$(\frac{3}{1})\frac{1}{3}y = (\frac{3}{1})5$
Step 3	Simplify.	$y = 15$
Step 4	Check.	$\frac{1}{3}(15) = 5$

Directions Solve each equation. Check your answer.

1. $\frac{1}{4}x = 1$ _____

2. $\frac{1}{8}w = 3$ _____

3. $\frac{1}{7}q = 2$ _____

4. $\frac{2}{5}r = 6$ _____

5. $\frac{4}{5}m = 20$ _____

6. $\frac{7}{8}k = 42$ _____

7. $\frac{2}{3}d = -10$ _____

8. $\frac{11}{16}y = 33$ _____

9. $\frac{1}{-5}a = -4$ _____

Directions Read the problem and follow the directions.

10. Spruceville received 35 inches of snow last winter, or $\frac{5}{8}$ of its average annual snowfall. What is Spruceville's average annual snowfall?

Let n stand for Spruceville's average annual snowfall:

$$\frac{5}{8}n = 35$$

How would you solve this equation? Circle the answer.

a. Subtract 35 and then multiply by $\frac{5}{8}$.

b. Multiply both sides by $\frac{8}{5}$.

c. Subtract $\frac{5}{8}$ from both sides.

Solving Equations—More Than One Step

EXAMPLE   Solve $2m - 7 = 1$ for m.

Step 1   Add 7 to both sides. $2m - 7 + (7) = 1 + (7)$ Simplify: $2m = 8$

Step 2   Divide both sides by 2. $\frac{2m}{2} = \frac{8}{2}$ Simplify: $m = 4$

Step 3   Check. $2(4) - 7 = 1$ Simplify: $1 = 1$

Directions   Solve each equation. Check your answer.

1. $4b + 1 = 17$ _____

2. $2c + 18 = 24$ _____

3. $7x - 2 = 5$ _____

4. $3p + 8 = 38$ _____

5. $8v - 1 = 39$ _____

6. $2w - 16 = 0$ _____

7. $5g + 5 = 35$ _____

Directions   One step is missing in the solution to each equation. In a complete sentence, write the missing step.

8. $7y - 4 = 10$

Step 1   Add 4 to both sides of the equation.

Step 2   _____

9. $2d + 1 = 19$

Step 1   _____

Step 2   Divide both sides of the equation by 2.

10. $3k + 3 = 12$

Step 1   Subtract 3 from both sides of the equation.

Step 2   _____

Equations Without Numbers

EXAMPLE $ax - b = c$ Solve for x.

Step 1	Write the equation.	$2x - 5 = 7$	$ax - b = c$
Step 2	Add 5 or b to both sides.	$2x - 5 + 5 = 7 + 5$	$ax - b + b = c + b$
		$2x = 12$	$ax = b + c$
Step 3	Divide each side by 2 or a.	$\frac{2x}{2} = \frac{12}{2}$	$\frac{ax}{a} = \frac{b+c}{a}$
Step 4	Check.	$x = 6$	$x = \frac{b+c}{a}$
		$2(6) - 5 = 7$	$a(\frac{b+c}{a}) - b = c$
		$7 = 7$	$(b + c) - b = c$
			$c = c$

Directions   Solve each equation for x. Check your answer.

1. $ax - c = b$ _____

2. $bc = ax$ _____

3. $x - b + a = c$ _____

4. $abx = -c$ _____

Directions   Follow the directions to solve the problem.

5. Center School has won two more soccer games than the combined wins of River School and Bluff School.

This statement can be turned into a mathematical equation.
- Let x stand for the number of games Center School has won.
- Let y stand for the number of games River School has won.
- Let z stand for the number of games Bluff School has won.
     $x = y + z + 2$

Solve the equation for z to show the number of soccer games Bluff School has won.

_____

_____

Formulas

EXAMPLE	Solve the formula for the perimeter of a triangle for *c*.

$$P = a + b + c$$
$$a + b + c = P$$
$$(a + b) + c - (a + b) = P - (a + b)$$
$$c = P - (a + b)$$

Directions Solve each equation.

1. $P = 6s$ for s _____

2. $A = \frac{1}{2}h(m + n)$ for m _____

3. $P = 2b + 2h$ for b _____

4. $A = lw$ for l _____

5. $P = a + b + c$ for b _____

6. $A = \frac{1}{2}h(m + n)$ for n _____

7. $V = hm$ for m _____

8. $P = 2b + 2h$ for h _____

Directions Answer the questions to solve the problem.

Mr. Jiang is building a deck on his house. He can calculate the perimeter of the deck using this formula:

$$P = 4s$$

9. Solve the equation to show the length of a side—that is, solve for *s*.

_____

_____

10. Is Mr. Jiang's deck in the shape of a square or a rectangle? Explain your answer.

_____

_____

_____

Name _____ Date _____ Period _____

Workbook Activity
Chapter 3, Lesson 9
33

The Pythagorean Theorem

EXAMPLE

Use the Pythagorean theorem: $c^2 = a^2 + b^2$

Find c when $a = 4$ and $b = 5$. Use a calculator, and round the answer to the nearest tenth.

$$c^2 = (4)^2 + (5)^2$$
$$c^2 = 16 + 25$$
$$c^2 = 41$$
$$c = \sqrt{41} = 6.403124 \qquad \text{Round off: 6.4}$$

Directions Use the Pythagorean theorem and a calculator to find the missing side of each triangle. Round to the nearest tenth.

1. $a = 2$ $b = 7$ $c = \square$ _____

2. $a = \square$ $b = 6$ $c = 10$ _____

3. $a = \square$ $b = 8$ $c = 14$ _____

4. $a = 9$ $b = \square$ $c = 36$ _____

Directions Solve the problem.

5. A sailboat has a sail in the shape of a right triangle. You know that side a is 2 m long and side b is 4 m long. How long is side c of the sail?

Substitute known values in the Pythagorean theorem and solve. Use your calculator and round to the nearest tenth.

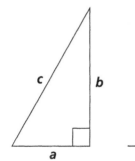

_____

Using the Pythagorean Theorem

EXAMPLE

The lengths of the sides of a triangle are 3 ft, 4 ft, and 5 ft. Is the triangle a right triangle?

When the lengths of the sides of a right triangle are given, the longest length is the hypotenuse. Substitute 3, 4, and 5 into the formula $a^2 + b^2 = c^2$.

$$a^2 + b^2 = c^2$$
$$3^2 + 4^2 = 5^2$$
$$9 + 16 = 25$$
$$25 = 25 \quad \text{True}$$

When the lengths of the sides of a triangle are 3 ft, 4 ft, and 5 ft, the triangle is a right triangle.

EXAMPLE

The lengths of the sides of a triangle are 10 cm, 13 cm, and 15 cm. Is the triangle a right triangle?

When the lengths of the sides of a right triangle are given, the longest length is the hypotenuse. Substitute 10, 13, and 15 into the formula $a^2 + b^2 = c^2$.

$$a^2 + b^2 = c^2$$
$$10^2 + 13^2 = 15^2$$
$$100 + 169 = 225$$
$$269 = 225 \quad \text{False}$$

When the lengths of the sides of a triangle are 10 cm, 13 cm, and 15 cm, the triangle is not a right triangle.

Directions The lengths of the sides of various triangles are given below. Is the triangle a right triangle?

1. 4 in., 5 in., 7 in. _____

2. 5 cm, 12 cm, 13 cm _____

3. 21 mm, 24 mm, 32 mm _____

4. 2 yd, 3 yd, $\sqrt{13}$ yd _____

5. 51 m, 68 m, 85 m _____

Inequalities on the Number Line

EXAMPLE Write a statement of inequality for the number line. Use *x* as the variable.

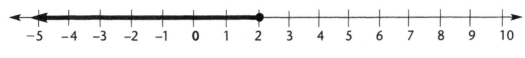

$x \le 2$

Directions Write a statement of inequality for each number line. Use *x* as the variable.

1.

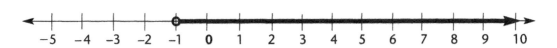

2.

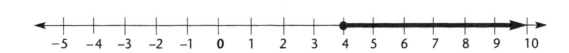

3.

4.

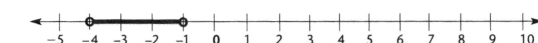

Directions Write *T* if the disjunction is True or *F* if it is False.

5. $3 \le 5$ _____   **8.** $-1 \ge 1$ _____

6. $8 \ge -3$ _____   **9.** $0 \ge -5$ _____

7. $2 \ge 4$ _____   **10.** $-2 \ge -14$ _____

Solving Inequalities with One Variable

EXAMPLE   Solve $x - 5 > 3$ for x.

       Step 1 Write the inequality. $x - 5 > 3$

       Step 2 Add 5 to both sides of the inequality. $x - 5 + 5 > 3 + 5$

       Step 3 Simplify. $x > 8$

       Note: For inequalities with addition, multiplication, or fractions, solve in the same way as for equations with the same operations.

Directions Solve each inequality.

1. $x - 3 > 0$ _____

2. $5d > 10$ _____

3. $k + 11 < 12$ _____

4. $4q > 48$ _____

5. $c + 3 \leq 40$ _____

6. $g - 1 < 6$ _____

7. $7p < 21$ _____

8. $w + 9 \geq 2$ _____

Directions Solve the problems.

9. A school has arranged teaching loads so that no teacher ever has more than 25 students. Describe the school's teaching load using an inequality and the variable t.

_____

10. The sponsor of a concert promises the concert singer a fee based on $5 per person in the audience. If attendance is below 200, however, the singer will be paid a minimum fee based on 200 seats filled. Using the variable f, write an inequality to represent the singer's minimum fee.

_____

Writing Equations—Odd and Even Integers

| EXAMPLE | Two times a number added to 4 is 14. What is the number? |

Step 1 Let n = the number.

Then $2n$ is "two times" the number.

Step 2 Write and solve the equation.

$$4 + 2n = 14$$
$$4 - 4 + 2n = 14 - 4$$
$$2n = 10$$
$$n = 5$$

Step 3 Check: $4 + 2(5) = 14$

$$14 = 14$$

Directions Write an equation for each statement. Use n as the variable.

1. Three times a number added to 2 is 5. _____

2. Four times a number decreased by 5 is 15. _____

3. Five added to 8 times a number is 53. _____

4. Seven times a number minus 2 is 40. _____

5. Eleven times a number added to 10 is 32. _____

6. Eight times a number decreased by 25 is −1. _____

7. Four added to 9 times a number is 76. _____

8. Ten times a number decreased by 1 is 99. _____

9. Nine times a number minus 14 is 22. _____

Directions Solve the problem.

10. A cook in a cafeteria has only 7 slices of rye bread left at closing time. An assistant immediately goes to a store and buys 4 identical loaves of sliced rye bread. With this additional supply, the cafeteria now has 79 slices of rye bread. How many slices are in one packaged loaf of rye bread?

_____

Using the 1% Solution to Solve Problems

EXAMPLE   A train has traveled 150 miles toward its destination.
This distance represents 30% of the total trip. What
will the total mileage be?

Step 1	30% of mileage = 150	Given.
Step 2	30% ÷ 30 = 150 ÷ 30	Divide both sides by 30 to solve for 1%.
	1% of mileage = 5	
Step 3	100% of mileage = 500	Multiply both sides by 100 to find the total mileage.

Directions   Use the 1% method to find a number when a given
percentage of the number is known.

1. 25% of a number is 200.   _____

2. 11% of a number is 33.   _____

3. 5% of a number is 35.   _____

4. 98% of a number is 294.   _____

5. 17% of a number is 153.   _____

6. 44% of a number is 88.   _____

7. 69% of a number is 69.   _____

8. 30% of a number is 90.   _____

Directions   Solve the problems.

9. At Mayville Community College, 490 students are enrolled in the
computer program. If 70% of the students in the college are in the
computer program, how many students does Mayville Community
College have in all?

_____

10. An airline reports that 9% of its flying customers last year were under
12 years of age. If 270,000 children under 12 years of age flew on the
airline's planes, how many customers did the airline have last year?

_____

Using the Percent Equation

EXAMPLE 30% of the pencils in a box of 20 pencils are red. How many red pencils are there?

Step 1 Write the percent equation. $(\frac{p}{100})(n) = r$

Step 2 Change the percent into a fraction. $p = 30$ $(\frac{30}{100})(n) = r$

Step 3 Write the total number. $n = 20$ $(\frac{30}{100})(20) = r$

Step 4 Simplify the fraction. $(\frac{3}{10})(20) = r$

Step 5 Solve the equation. $(\frac{3}{10})(20) = 6$

30% of 20 is 6. There are 6 red pencils in the box.

Directions Use the percent equation to find the percent of each given number.

1. 10% of 40 _____

2. 20% of 60 _____

3. 50% of 34 _____

4. 25% of 200 _____

5. 75% of 16 _____

6. 21% of 100 _____

7. 50% of 18 _____

8. 35% of 200 _____

9. 13% of 1,000 _____

Directions Solve the problem.

10. Last summer, Jan gave away 15% of the tomatoes she raised in her garden. Jan picked a total of 120 tomatoes. How many did she give away?

_____

_____

Name ___ Date ___ Period ___

Using Percents

This chart displays population data of the world's ten largest cities.

Population of the World's Ten Largest Cities			
Rank	City/Country	Population 1994	Projected Population 2015
1	Tokyo, Japan	26,518,000	28,700,000
2	New York City, U.S.	16,271,000	17,600,000
3	São Paulo, Brazil	16,110,000	20,800,000
4	Mexico City, Mexico	15,525,000	18,800,000
5	Shanghai, China	14,709,000	23,400,000
6	Bombay (Mumbai), India	14,496,000	27,400,000
7	Los Angeles, U.S.	12,232,000	14,300,000
8	Beijing, China	12,030,000	19,400,000
9	Calcutta, India	11,485,000	17,600,000
10	Seoul, South Korea	11,451,000	13,100,000

Directions The chart shows the 1994 population in each city and a projection of the population in the year 2015. Use the chart to answer these questions.

1. In which city is the population expected to increase the most? By how many people is the population expected to increase? ___

2. In which city is the population expected to increase the least? By how many people is the population expected to increase? ___

3. Which city is expected to experience the greatest percent of increase? By what percent, to the nearest whole number, is the population expected to increase? ___

4. Which city is expected to experience the least percent of increase? By what percent, to the nearest whole number, is the population expected to increase? ___

5. In 1996, the population of the world was 5,771,938,000 people. By 2020, the world's population is projected to increase to 7,601,786,000 people. By what percent, to the nearest whole number, is the population of the world expected to increase between 1996 and 2020? ___

Solving Distance, Rate, and Time Problems

EXAMPLE   The distance formula is $d = rt$.

   d stands for **distance**, r for **rate** of speed, and t for **time**.

Find d when $r = 20$ kilometers per hour (km/h) and $t = 2$ hours.

Solve: $d = (20)(2) = 40$ kilometers

Use $r = \frac{d}{t}$ to solve for rate of speed.

Find r when $d = 33$ miles and $t = 3$ hours.

Solve: $r = \frac{33}{3} = 11$ miles per hour (mph)

Use $t = \frac{d}{r}$ to solve for total time.

Find t when $d = 450$ kilometers and $r = 90$ km/h.

Solve: $t = \frac{450}{90} = 5$ hours

Directions   Use the appropriate version of the distance formula to find
the unknown value.

1. $d = ?$ $r = 5$ mph $t = \frac{1}{2}$ hour   Answer in miles.   _____

2. $d = ?$ $r = 38$ km/h $t = 3$ hours   Answer in kilometers.   _____

3. $d = 90$ miles $r = 60$ mph $t = ?$ Answer in hours.   _____

4. $d = 1,968$ kilometers $r = ?$ $t = 24$ hours   Answer in km/h.   _____

5. $d = 54$ miles $r = 18$ mph $t = ?$ Answer in hours.   _____

6. $d = ?$ $r = 27$ km/h $t = \frac{1}{3}$ hour   Answer in kilometers.   _____

7. $d = 332$ kilometers $r = ?$ $t = 4$ hours   Answer in km/h.   _____

8. $d = 14$ miles $r = 70$ mph $t = ?$ Answer in hours.   _____

9. $d = 1,233$ miles $r = ?$ $t = 3$ hours   Answer in mph.   _____

10. $d = ?$ $r = 96$ km/h $t = \frac{3}{4}$ hour   Answer in kilometers.   _____

Using a Common Unit—Cents

EXAMPLE   In algebra equations, represent money as cent values.

penny = 1 cent   dime = 10 cents   dollar = 100 cents

nickel = 5 cents   quarter = 25 cents

Change dollar amounts into cents by multiplying by 100.

Suppose you have $3.00. How many cents do you have?

3.00 • 100 = 300 cents

To represent money amounts, multiply the number of coins by value.

Suppose you have n nickels + twice as many ($2n$) dimes. What is the money value?

$n(5) + 2n(10)$ or $5n + 20n$

Directions Write the value of each amount of money in cents.

1. $1.92 _____

2. $7.46 _____

3. $11.00 _____

4. $2.25 _____

5. $22.95 _____

6. $0.89 _____

Directions For each group of coins, choose the expression that gives the total money value of the coins in cents. Circle the letter of your choice.

7. n quarters plus twice as many dimes

   a. $n(25) + 2n(10)$ **b.** $n + 2n$

8. n nickels plus half as many quarters

   a. $n + \frac{1}{2}n$ **b.** $n(5) + \frac{1}{2}n(25)$

9. n dimes plus 4 times as many pennies

   a. $n(1) + 4n(10)$ **b.** $n(10) + 4n(1)$

Directions Write an expression for the money value of the given coins, in cents.

10. n dimes $+ \frac{1}{5}$ as many quarters _____

Calculating Simple Interest

EXAMPLE

- Use the formula $I = prt$ to calculate simple interest.

  How much interest will $300 at 6% interest earn in 1 year?

  $I = \$300(0.06)(1) = \$18$

- Use the formula $p = \frac{I}{rt}$ to solve for p and calculate principal.

  Find the principal in an account that has a rate of 5% and earns $75 interest in 2 years.

  $p = \frac{\$75}{(0.05)(2)} = \$750$

- Use the formula $r = \frac{I}{pt}$ to solve for r and calculate rate of interest.

  What is the rate of interest if $1,000 earns $240 interest in 3 years?

  $r = \frac{\$240}{(\$1,000)(3)} = 0.08$, or 8%

Directions Calculate interest on the given principal, rate, and time.

1. $p = \$200$ $r = 3\%$ $t = 1$ year   _____

2. $p = \$720$ $r = 4\%$ $t = 1$ year   _____

3. $p = \$1,400$ $r = 7\%$ $t = 2$ years   _____

Directions Calculate principal from the given interest, rate, and time.

4. $I = \$90$ $r = 6\%$ $t = 3$ years   _____

5. $I = \$27$ $r = 3\%$ $t = 1$ year   _____

6. $I = \$256$ $r = 8\%$ $t = 1$ year   _____

Directions Calculate rate from the given interest, principal, and time.

7. $I = \$63$ $p = \$700$ $t = 1$ year   _____

8. $I = \$24$ $p = \$150$ $t = 4$ years   _____

9. $I = \$48$ $p = \$960$ $t = 1$ year   _____

Directions Solve the problem.

10. For 2 years, Will kept $655 in a savings account that earned 4% annual interest. How much interest did Will earn?

Deriving a Formula for Mixture Problems

EXAMPLE   Use this formula to determine the cost of a mixture:

Price per pound = $\frac{\text{cost of total mixture}}{\text{number of pounds}}$

Peanuts cost $3.00 per pound. Cashews cost $6.00 per pound.
Suppose you mix 4 pounds of peanuts with 2 pounds of cashews.
What will the mixture cost, per pound?

Price per pound = $\frac{4(\$3) + 2(\$6)}{4 + 2} = \frac{\$24}{6} = \$4$

Directions   Use the information in each table to answer the questions that follow it. The formula you will need is in the example on this page.

Item	Cost per pound	Number of pounds
beans	$2.00	7
dried tomatoes	$6.00	1

1. Fill in the formula with this data. _____

2. Find the cost of this mixture. _____

Item	Cost per pound	Number of pounds
popcorn	$9.00	2
peanuts	$3.00	1

3. Fill in the formula with this data. _____

4. Find the cost of this mixture. _____

Directions   Solve the problem.

5. Suppose a grocery store mixes 4 pounds of oat cereal with 1 pound of almonds. The oat cereal costs $1.20 per pound, and the almonds cost $4.80 per pound. What should the mixture cost per pound?

_____

Ratio and Proportion

EXAMPLE

$\frac{2}{3} = \frac{4}{6}$ because the cross products are equal.

$\frac{2}{3} \times \frac{4}{6}$ $2 \cdot 6 = 4 \cdot 3$, so $12 = 12$

Find the missing term in the proportion $\frac{2}{5} = \frac{x}{10}$ by making an equation from the cross products. Then solve the equation.

$\frac{2}{5} \times \frac{x}{10}$ $20 = 5x$ or $5x = 20$

$x = 4$

Therefore, $\frac{2}{5} = \frac{4}{10}$

Directions Tell whether each equation is a proportion. Prove your answer.

1. $\frac{1}{4} = \frac{2}{8}$ _____

2. $\frac{1}{7} = \frac{2}{14}$ _____

3. $\frac{2}{7} = \frac{3}{14}$ _____

4. $\frac{4}{5} = \frac{15}{20}$ _____

5. $\frac{3}{4} = \frac{12}{16}$ _____

6. $\frac{3}{10} = \frac{6}{30}$ _____

7. $\frac{1}{3} = \frac{2}{6}$ _____

8. $\frac{1}{6} = \frac{3}{18}$ _____

Directions Find the missing term in each proportion.

9. $\frac{1}{3} = \frac{x}{15}$ $x =$ _____

10. $\frac{2}{4} = \frac{6}{x}$ $x =$ _____

11. $\frac{2}{9} = \frac{x}{27}$ $x =$ _____

12. $\frac{1}{x} = \frac{2}{10}$ $x =$ _____

13. $\frac{2}{3} = \frac{4}{x}$ $x =$ _____

14. $\frac{2}{7} = \frac{x}{14}$ $x =$ _____

15. $\frac{x}{5} = \frac{3}{15}$ $x =$ _____

Exponents

EXAMPLE   To multiply terms with exponents, add the exponents.

$$n^2 \cdot n^2 = n^{2+2} = n^4$$

To raise a power to a power, multiply the exponents.

$$(n^2)^3 = n^{2 \cdot 3} = n^6$$

To divide terms with exponents, subtract the exponents.

$$n^5 \div n^2 = n^{5-2} = n^3 \quad \text{(Note: } n \neq 0.\text{)}$$

Directions   Use the rule for dividing terms with exponents to find each
                 answer.

1. $4^3 \div 4^2$ _____

2. $y^5 \div y^3, y \neq 0$ _____

3. $m^8 \div m^4, m \neq 0$ _____

4. $r^9 \div r, r \neq 0$ _____

5. $6^5 \div 6$ _____

6. $(j+k)^4 \div (j+k)^2, (j+k) \neq 0$ _____

7. $10^8 \div 10^8$ _____

8. $w^7 \div w^7, w \neq 0$ _____

Directions   Answer the questions to solve the problem.

A square has a side s that is 3^2 m long. The formula for area of a
square is $A = s^2$. Fill in the blank to show how to calculate the area
of this square.

$$s = 3^2 \text{ m}$$

$$\boxed{ s }$$

9. Area = (_____)^2 square m

Next calculate the area of the square by using the rule for raising a
power to a power. (See the previous answer.)

10. Area = _____ square m

Negative Exponents

EXAMPLE	Rewrite $\frac{1}{10^2}$ with a negative exponent: 10^{-2}.

Rewrite $\frac{1}{x^3}$ with a negative exponent, $x \neq 0$: x^{-3}.

Rewrite 2^{-5} with a positive exponent: $\frac{1}{2^5}$.

Rewrite n^{-2} with a positive exponent, $n \neq 0$: $\frac{1}{n^2}$.

Directions Rewrite using a negative exponent.

1. $\frac{1}{8^2}$ _____

2. $\frac{1}{2}$ _____

3. $\frac{3^2}{3^3}$ _____

4. $\frac{1}{10^5}$ _____

5. $\frac{10^3}{10^6}$ _____

6. $\frac{1}{c^2}, c \neq 0$ _____

7. $8^2 \div 8^5$ _____

8. $\frac{1}{y^7}, y \neq 0$ _____

9. $\frac{1}{18^3}$ _____

10. $\frac{1}{(3j - 2k)^4}$ _____

Directions Rewrite using a positive exponent.

11. 5^{-3} _____

12. 10^{-3} _____

13. x^{-5} _____

14. 8^{-5} _____

15. y^{-7} _____

16. 10^{-7} _____

17. $(2d + 3k)^{-3}$ _____

18. n^{-4} _____

19. 7^{-2} _____

20. $(m - 3n)^{-2}$ _____

Directions Simplify each power of 2.

21. $2^2 =$ _____

22. $2^1 =$ _____

23. $2^0 =$ _____

24. $2^{-1} =$ _____

25. $2^{-2} =$ _____

Exponents and Scientific Notation

EXAMPLE   Write 500.37 and 0.0041 in scientific notation.

Step 1	500.37	0.0041
Step 2	Count decimal places: 2 to the left.	Count decimal places: 3 to the right.
Step 3	$5.0037 \cdot 10^2$	$4.1 \cdot 10^{-3}$
	(Rule: Use a positive exponent if the decimal point moved left.)	(Rule: Use a negative exponent if the decimal point moved right.)

Directions Write each number in scientific notation.

1. 29,900 _____

2. 0.0016 _____

3. 0.0199 _____

4. 883 _____

5. 11,000 _____

6. 2,230,000 _____

7. 0.001 _____

8. 0.0000314 _____

9. 0.0009999 _____

10. 304,922 _____

11. 17,250 _____

12. 29,839,250 _____

13. 0.0000000033 _____

14. 3,000,000,000 _____

15. 222.6 _____

16. 0.0000002 _____

17. 260,000,000 _____

18. 0.00007 _____

Directions Solve the problems.

19. A certain bacteria cell is 0.0008 mm thick. Write this measurement in scientific notation.

_____

20. Dinosaurs became extinct (that is, died out) about 65 million years ago. This number is written out as 65,000,000. Rewrite it in scientific notation.

_____

Computing in Scientific Notation

EXAMPLE   Multiply: $0.005 \cdot 7{,}150{,}000$

   Step 1 $0.005 = 5.0 \cdot 10^{-3}$ $7{,}150{,}000 = 7.15 \cdot 10^{6}$

   Step 2 $(5.0 \cdot 10^{-3})(7.15 \cdot 10^{6}) = (5.0 \cdot 7.15)(10^{-3} \cdot 10^{6})$

   Step 3 $(35.75)(10^{-3\,+\,6}) = (35.75)(10^{3})$

   Step 4 $(3.575)(10)(10^{3}) = (3.575)(10^{1\,+\,3}) = (3.575)(10^{4})$

Directions Find each product. Write the answer in scientific notation.

1. $0.0007 \cdot 190$ _____

2. $2{,}400{,}000 \cdot 0.006$ _____

3. $0.0018 \cdot 0.054$ _____

4. $18{,}500 \cdot 2{,}250$ _____

5. $3{,}600 \cdot 0.00000005$ _____

EXAMPLE   Divide: $110{,}000{,}000 \div 250$

   Step 1 $110{,}000{,}000 = 1.1 \cdot 10^{8}$ $250 = 2.5 \cdot 10^{2}$

   Step 2 $\dfrac{1.1 \cdot 10^{8}}{2.5 \cdot 10^{2}} = (1.1 \div 2.5)(10^{8} \div 10^{2})$

   Step 3 $(0.44)(10^{8\,-\,2}) = 0.44(10^{6})$

   Step 4 $4.4(10^{-1})(10^{6}) = (4.4)(10^{-1\,+\,6}) = (4.4)(10^{5})$

Directions Find each quotient. Write the answer in scientific notation.

6. $93{,}000{,}000 \div 3{,}100$ _____

7. $7{,}700 \div 0.0025$ _____

8. $1{,}008 \div 900{,}000$ _____

9. $0.00086 \div 0.025$ _____

10. $19.8 \div 0.0003$ _____

Defining and Naming Polynomials

EXAMPLE

The chart summarizes the kinds of polynomials.
The greatest power of a variable is called *the degree of a polynomial.*

Expression	Name of the Polynomial	Degree
$2y^2$	monomial	2
$2y^2 + 5$	binomial	2
$2y^2 - 3y + 5$	trinomial	2
$y^3 + 2y^2 - 3y + 5$	polynomial	3

Directions Fill in the missing data in the chart. Write on each numbered blank.

Expression	Name of the Polynomial	Degree
$3n^2 + 2n$	1. _____	2
$k^3 - 2k^2 + k - 4$	polynomial	2. _____
$5x$	monomial	3. _____
$3x^2$	4. _____	2
$7y^2 + 4y - 5$	trinomial	5. _____
$n^3 + n^2 - 8n - 8$	6. _____	7. _____
$93n$	8. _____	1
$11k^2 - 2k + 17$	9. _____	10. _____
$b^2 + 4$	11. _____	12. _____

Directions Each expression is described incorrectly. Write what is wrong with the description.

13. $k + 5$ "binomial in k, degree 2" _____

14. $y^2 - 4$ "trinomial in y, degree 2" _____

15. $r^3 - r^2 - 3r + 7$ "polynomial in x, degree 3" _____

Adding and Subtracting Polynomials

EXAMPLE

Add $(2x^3 + 4x^2 + 8)$ and $(x^3 - 2x^2 - x + 3)$.

$$
\begin{array}{rrrr}
2x^3 & + 4x^2 & & + 8 \\
+ \quad x^3 & - 2x^2 & - x & + 3 \\
\hline
3x^3 & + 2x^2 & - x & + 11
\end{array}
$$

Subtract $(2x^3 - 4x - 1)$ from $(4x^3 + 7x^2 - 3x + 4)$.

Find the opposite of the expression to be subtracted:

$$(-1)(2x^3 - 4x - 1) \quad = \quad -2x^3 + 4x + 1$$

$$
\begin{array}{rrrrr}
\textbf{Add:} & 4x^3 & + 7x^2 & - 3x & + 4 \\
+ & -2x^3 & & + 4x & + 1 \\
\hline
& 2x^3 & + 7x^2 & + x & + 5
\end{array}
$$

Directions Find each sum.

1. $(5k^3 - 9k^2 + 12k - 3)$ and $(k^3 + 10k^2 + k + 14)$ _____

2. $(3y^4 + 2y^2 - 7y)$ and $(5y^3 - 2y^2 + 2y + 9)$ _____

Directions Find each difference. Remember to add the opposite.

3. $(4n^2 - 8n + 3) - (3n^2 + 5n - 4)$ _____

4. $(6x^4 - x^3 + 12x - 16) - (5x^3 + 2)$ _____

Directions Solve the problem.

5. A nut company will close one of its two stores and combine all of the inventory (the nuts in stock) from the two stores. The following polynomials give the number of bags of dry-roasted peanuts in each store:

Lakewood store: $x^2 + 4x - 2$

Downtown store: $3x^2 - x + 4$

Find the combined inventory of the dry-roasted peanuts.

_____

Multiplying Polynomials

EXAMPLE   Multiply $(n + 2)(n - 3)$. Use the distributive property.

$$(n + 2)(n - 3) \ = \ n(n - 3) + 2(n - 3)$$
$$= \ n^2 - 3n + 2n - 6$$
$$= \ n^2 - n - 6$$

Directions Find each product.

1. $(k + 4)(3k - 6)$ _____

2. $(-2x + 5)(-x - 10)$ _____

3. $(c^2 + c)^2$ _____

4. $(d^2)(d + 5)$ _____

5. $(y + 9)(y^2 - 2y + 6)$ _____

6. $(n - 3)(n^3 + 6n - 3)$ _____

7. $(w^3 + 1)(w^2 - 4)$ _____

8. $(-2x - 5)(3x^5 + x^4 - 4x^3 + 6x^2)$ _____

9. $(c^3)(c^2 - 3c + 9)$ _____

10. $(2k + 7)(2k - 5)$ _____

11. $(m - 3)(m^4 - 3m^3 - 7m - 1)$ _____

12. $(8b + 3)(2b - 9)$ _____

13. $(k^3)(k^6 + 2k^5 - 3k^4 - 8k^3 + 4k^2 - 9k - 9)$ _____

14. $(7n - 4)(3n^3 - 8n^2 - 5n + 8)$ _____

Directions Solve the problem.

15. A machine in a factory turns out a large metal grid (a crisscross or checkerboard pattern), which later gets cut into small pieces for computer parts. The measurements of this large grid are as follows:

length: $(3x + 12)$ width: $(2x - 3)$

Find the area of this grid, using the formula: Area = length • width.

_____

Special Polynomial Products

EXAMPLE

Each of these polynomial products forms a pattern.

$(a + b)^2 \quad = (a + b)(a + b) \quad = a(a + b) + b(a + b) \quad = a^2 + 2ab + b^2$

$(a - b)^2 \quad = (a - b)(a - b) \quad = a(a - b) - b(a - b) \quad = a^2 - 2ab + b^2$

$(a + b)(a - b) = a(a - b) + b(a - b) \quad = a^2 - b^2$

$(a + b)^3 \quad = (a + b)(a + b)(a + b) = (a + b)[(a + b)(a + b)] = a^3 + 3a^2b + 3ab^2 + b^3$

Directions Study each product. Decide what polynomials were multiplied to give the product. Use the example above as a guide. Write your answer in the blank.

1. $m^2 + 2mn + n^2$ _____

2. $j^2 - k^2$ _____

3. $x^2 + 2xy + y^2$ _____

4. $c^3 + 3c^2d + 3cd^2 + d^3$ _____

5. $w^2 - x^2$ _____

6. $g^2 - 2gh + h^2$ _____

Directions Find each product. Compare your solutions with the patterns in the example, above.

7. $(p + r)(p - r)$ _____

8. $(f + g)^2$ _____

9. $(y + z)^3$ _____

10. $(a + d)(a - d)$ _____

11. $(p - q)(p - q)$ _____

12. $(t + u)(t + u)(t + u)$ _____

13. $(n + p)(n + p)$ _____

14. $(c - d)^2$ _____

15. $(k + m)(k - m)$ _____

Exponents and Complex Fractions

EXAMPLE

It is possible to simplify complex fractions that contain exponents.

Simplify. $\dfrac{\frac{1}{a^2}}{\frac{b^2}{a}}$

Step 1 Rewrite the complex fraction horizontally. Recall that the fraction bar separating the numerator from the denominator means "divide."

$$\frac{\frac{1}{a^2}}{\frac{b^2}{a}} = \frac{1}{a^2} \div \frac{b^2}{a}$$

Step 2 Multiply each term in the expression by the reciprocal of the divisor.

$$\frac{1}{a^2} \div \frac{b^2}{a} = \left(\frac{1}{a^2}\right)\left(\frac{a}{b^2}\right) \div \left(\frac{b^2}{a}\right)\left(\frac{a}{b^2}\right)$$

Step 3 Simplify.

$$\left(\frac{1}{a^2}\right)\left(\frac{a}{b^2}\right) \div \left(\frac{b^2}{a}\right)\left(\frac{a}{b^2}\right) = \left(\frac{1}{a^2}\right)\left(\frac{a}{b^2}\right) = \left(\frac{1}{ab^2}\right)$$

Directions Simplify these complex fractions.

1. $\dfrac{\frac{1}{b^2}}{\frac{a}{b^2}}$

4. $\dfrac{\frac{1}{g^3}}{\frac{1}{g}}$

7. $\dfrac{\frac{24cde^4}{d}}{\frac{8e^3}{d}}$

10. $\dfrac{\frac{8c^2}{9b^5d}}{\frac{2cd}{b^3}}$

2. $\dfrac{\frac{c^2}{2}}{\frac{2}{d}}$

5. $\dfrac{\frac{2xy^2}{z}}{\frac{xy}{z}}$

8. $\dfrac{\frac{3r^2st^2}{u}}{\frac{r}{u}}$

3. $\dfrac{\frac{5}{a^3}}{\frac{5}{b}}$

6. $\dfrac{\frac{10m^3n}{p}}{\frac{2p^2}{n^2}}$

9. $\dfrac{\frac{12g^4hi^2}{ah}}{\frac{gh^2}{ai}}$

Dividing a Polynomial by a Monomial

EXAMPLE   Find the quotient of $(3x^3 - 6x^2 + 9x) \div 3x$.

Step 1 Rewrite the problem. $\frac{3x^3 - 6x^2 + 9x}{3x}$

Step 2 Divide each term of the numerator by the term in the denominator.

$\frac{3x^3}{3x}$ $\frac{6x^2}{3x}$ $\frac{9x}{3x}$

$= x^2 - 2x + 3$ (quotient)

Step 3 Check by multiplying quotient by divisor. The answer should be the dividend.

$(x^2 - 2x + 3)(3x) = 3x^3 - 6x^2 + 9x$ (dividend)

Directions Find each quotient. Check your work using multiplication.

1. $(15n^2 - 5n + 45) \div 5$ _____

2. $(16y^3 - 4y) \div (4y)$ _____

3. $(2k^7 - 4k^6 + 16k^5 - 22k^3 - 6k^2) \div (2k^2)$ _____

Directions Solve the problems.

4. An engineer in a paper-clip factory represents the number of paper clips that come out of a machine in one hour by the following polynomial expression: $2x^5 + 4x^4 + 16x^2 - 128x$. The paper clips are packed in boxes, each of which holds $2x$ paper clips. How many boxes will be filled by an hour's run of the paper-clip machine?

_____

5. A textile factory produces a bolt (roll) of cloth 40 yards long. The expression $16k^4 + 8k^3 + 24k^2 - 32k$ gives the number of threads in this bolt of cloth. If the bolt is cut into 8 equal pieces of cloth, how many threads will each piece have?

_____

Dividing a Polynomial by a Binomial

EXAMPLE   Find the quotient of $(x^2 - 3x - 5) \div (x + 1)$.

$$
\begin{array}{r}
x - 4 \\
x + 1 \overline{)x^2 - 3x - 5} \\
\underline{-(x^2 + x)} \\
-4x - 5 \\
\underline{-(-4x - 4)} \\
-1 \quad \text{remainder}
\end{array}
$$

Check by multiplication: $(x + 1)(x - 4) - 1 = x^2 - 3x - 5$

Directions   Find each quotient. Identify any remainder.

1. $(2x^2 - x - 15) \div (2x + 5)$ _____

2. $(14a^2 - 26a - 4) \div (7a + 1)$ _____

3. $(5y^2 + 4y - 12) \div (y + 2)$ _____

4. $(3d^2 - 3d - 5) \div (d + 2)$ _____

Directions   Tell what is wrong with the following division work. Show
how to correct the error.

5.

$$
\begin{array}{r}
x^4 \\
x + 3 \overline{)x^5 + 3x - 9} \\
\underline{x^5 + 3x^4} \\
?
\end{array}
$$

_____

_____

_____

_____

Polynomials in Two or More Variables

EXAMPLE   Evaluate $P(x, y) = x^2 + xy + y^2$ for $x = 2$ and $y = -2$

     Step 1   Substitute the variables with their values.

        $P(2, -2) = (2)^2 + (2)(-2) + (-2)^2$

     Step 2   Follow the order of operations.

        $4 + -4 + 4$

     Step 3   Add.

        $4 + -4 + 4 = 4$

        $P(x, y) = 4$

Directions   Evaluate $P(x, y) = x^2 + xy + y^2$ for each set of values.

1. $x = 1, y = -2$ _____

2. $x = -1, y = 6$ _____

3. $x = \frac{1}{3}, y = -3$ _____

4. $x = -6, y = 5$ _____

5. $x = \frac{1}{2}, y = 8$ _____

Directions   Evaluate $P(x, y) = x^3y^2 + x^2y + xy^3$ at

6. $P(1, 2)$ _____

7. $P(-3, -2)$ _____

8. $P(7, 0)$ _____

9. $P(8, 2)$ _____

10. $P(-1, -5)$ _____

Directions   Evaluate $P(x, y, z) = x^3yz^2 + x^2y^2z^2 + xy^3 + yz$ for

11. $x = 1, y = 2, z = 1$ _____

12. $x = 1, y = 0, z = 4$ _____

13. $x = 2, y = -1, z = 3$ _____

14. $x = 0, y = 5, z = -1$ _____

15. $x = 2, y = -4, z = 0$ _____

Greatest Common Factor

EXAMPLE

Find the GCF.   140 and 56 $49k^4$ and $21k^2$

Step 1 Write the $140 = 2 \cdot 2 \cdot 5 \cdot 7$ $49k^4 = 7 \cdot 7 \cdot k \cdot k \cdot k \cdot k$
factorizations. $56 = 2 \cdot 2 \cdot 2 \cdot 7$ $21k^2 = 3 \cdot 7 \cdot k \cdot k$

Step 2 Identify common $2 \cdot 2 \cdot 7$ $7 \cdot k \cdot k$
prime factors.

Step 3 Write the GCF as a $2^2 \cdot 7 = 28$ $7k^2$
product.

Directions   Find the GCF for these groups of integers.

1. 60, 126 _____

2. 63, 70 _____

3. 45, 225 _____

4. 64, 114 _____

5. 42, 90 _____

Directions   Find the GCF for these groups of expressions.

6. $14x^5y^4, 7xy^3$ _____

7. $21j^3k^4, 54j^2k^6$ _____

8. $4a^3b^2, 18a^2b$ _____

9. $25m^6n, 30m^5n^2$_____

Directions   Solve the problem.

10. Dad just had a birthday. *Before* this birthday, dividing Dad's age by 2 left a remainder of 1. How do you know that Dad's new age is *not* a prime number?

_____

_____

_____

Factoring Polynomials

EXAMPLE   Factor $35x^3y^2 - 14x^2y^3$.

Step 1 Find the GCF:

$35x^3y^2 = 5 \cdot 7 \cdot x \cdot x \cdot x \cdot y \cdot y$

$14x^2y^3 = 2 \cdot 7 \cdot x \cdot x \cdot \quad y \cdot y \cdot y$ The GCF is $7x^2y^2$.

Step 2 Rewrite the expression using the GCF.

$35x^3y^2 - 14x^2y^3 = 7x^2y^2(5x)(1) - 7x^2y^2(2)(1)(y)$

$= 7x^2y^2(5x - 2y)$ by the distributive property

Step 3 Check. $7x^2y^2(5x - 2y) = 35x^3y^2 - 14x^2y^3$

Directions Find the GCF and factor these expressions.

1. $6a^2 + 9a$ _____

2. $2b^4 - 4b^2$ _____

3. $4d^2 + 8d - 2cd$ _____

4. $6x^3 - 9x^2y$ _____

5. $12a^2 - 3ab + 9a^2b^2$ _____

6. $j^2k^2 - jk$ _____

7. $12xyz^3 - 18xy^2z^2$ _____

8. $12m^3n^2p + 6m^2np - 3mp$ _____

Directions Solve the problems.

9. Suppose you have the following in your fruit bowl:

• x apples   • $6x$ peaches   • $2x^2$ pears

In all, you have $2x^2 + 7x$ pieces of fruit. Factor this expression.

_____

10. With the same contents in your fruit bowl, suppose you eat all of the x apples? Write an expression to represent the fruit you will now have left. Can this expression be factored? If it can, factor it.

_____

▶ Algebra

Factoring Trinomials: $x^2 + bx + c$

EXAMPLE

Factor $a^2 + 2a - 15$.

Step 1 $a^2 + 2a - 15 = (\square + \square)(\square - \square)$

Step 2 $a^2 + 2a - 15 = (a + \square)(a - \square)$ to give a^2

Step 3   Find factors of -15 whose sum is 2.

         $(5)(-3) = -15$, and $(5) + (-3) = 2$

         $a^2 + 2a - 15 = (a + 5)(a - 3)$

Step 4   Check by multiplying.
         $(a + 5)(a - 3) = a^2 + 2a - 15$

Directions   Factor the expressions. Check by multiplying.

1. $y^2 + 7y + 12$ _____

2. $w^2 - 4w - 21$ _____

3. $b^2 - 9b + 14$ _____

4. $x^2 - 11x + 18$ _____

5. $n^2 - 7n + 12$ _____

6. $z^2 - z - 30$ _____

7. $d^2 + 5d + 6$ _____

8. $a^2 - 5a - 50$ _____

9. $m^2 - 2m - 15$ _____

Directions   Solve the problem.

10. A grid (checkerboard pattern) is printed on each sheet of graph paper produced in a paper factory. The total number of squares on the printed grid is $x^2 - 6x - 27$. What is the length, in squares, of each side of the grid? (Hint: factor the trinomial.)

     _____

Factoring Trinomials: $ax^2 + bx + c$

EXAMPLE   Factor $3x^2 + 13x + 4$.

Step 1 $3x^2 + 13x + 4 = (\Box x + \Box)(\Box x + \Box)$ to give x^2

Step 2 Find factors of 3 and 4 whose sum is 13.

Factors of 3 = (1)(3)   Factors of 4 = (1)(2)(2)

After trying out the possible combinations, the following factors of the trinomial are found: $(3x + 1)(x + 4)$

Step 3 Check by multiplying.

$(3x + 1)(x + 4) = 3x^2 + 13x + 4$

Directions Factor these expressions.

1. $3a^2 + 4a + 1$ _____

2. $3x^2 - 4x - 4$ _____

3. $6d^2 - d - 15$ _____

4. $8x^2 - 18x + 9$ _____

5. $4n^2 + 13n + 3$ _____

6. $2y^2 - 7y + 3$ _____

7. $4x^2 + 11x - 3$ _____

8. $2n^2 - 5n + 3$ _____

9. $6b^2 + 7b - 20$ _____

Directions Solve the problem.

10. A pretzel-maker fills identical bags with an equal number of pretzels. In one hour, the pretzel-maker bags $(4k^2 + 17k + 18)$ pretzels in all. Factor this trinomial to find the number of bags (larger factor) and the number of pretzels per bag (smaller factor).

_____

Factoring Expressions: $a^2 - b^2$

EXAMPLE

Find the factors of $x^2 - 4$.

Step 1 Find the square roots of x^2 and 4.

$\sqrt{x^2} = x$ and $\sqrt{4} = 2$

Step 2 Place the values in the model. $a^2 - b^2 = (a + b)(a - b)$.

$x^2 - 4 = (x + 2)(x - 2)$

Step 3 Check by multiplying. $(x + 2)(x - 2) = x^2 - 4$

Directions Factor these expressions. Check your answers.

1. $y^2 - 144$ _____

2. $x^2 - 16$ _____

3. $w^2 - 400$ _____

4. $16b^2 - 81$ _____

5. $9x^2 - 4y^2$ _____

6. $4m^2 - 9n^2$ _____

7. $j^4 - k^2$ _____

8. $a^2b^2 - 100$ _____

9. $25c^2 - 169$ _____

10. $36n^4 - 25p^2$ _____

11. $484x^2 - 900y^2$ _____

12. $36a^8 - 49b^8$ _____

13. $49k^{16} - 25k^2$ _____

14. $121n^2 - 49p^2$ _____

Directions Solve the problem.

15. A town has an exactly rectangular shape. If the town's area is $(p^2 - 121)$ square kilometers, what is the length of the town border on each side of the rectangle it forms?

_____

Factoring Expressions: $a^2 + 2ab + b^2$

EXAMPLE   Find the factors of $n^2 + 8n + 16$.

Model for factoring: $a^2 + 2ab + b^2 = (a + b)^2$

Step 1 Assign values to n^2.

$a^2 = n^2$ or $a = \sqrt{n^2}$

$b^2 = 16$ or $b = \sqrt{16}$

$2ab = 2(n \cdot 4) = 8n$

Step 2 Place the values in the model.

$n^2 + 8n + 16 = (n + 4)^2$

Step 3 Check by multiplication.

$(n + 4)(n + 4) = n^2 + 8n + 16$

Directions Find the factors of each polynomial. Check your answers.

1. $r^2 + 10r + 25$ _____

2. $b^2 + 20b + 100$ _____

3. $k^2 + 2k + 1$ _____

4. $y^2 + 14y + 49$ _____

5. $x^2 + 4xy + 4y^2$ _____

6. $9v^2 + 42vw + 49w^2$ _____

7. $c^2 + 2cd + d^2$ _____

8. $4m^2 + 28mn + 49n^2$ _____

Directions Solve the problems.

9. A square parking lot has a surface area of $(w^4 - 2w^2x + x^2)$ square feet. Factor this trinomial to find the length of one side in feet.

_____

10. The surface of a square window pane is $(k^2 + 8k + 16)$ cm^2 in area. Factor this trinomial to find the length of one side of the pane in cm.

_____

Zero as a Factor

EXAMPLE Find the value of the variable in each example.

$3n = 0$ Since $3 \neq 0$, n must be 0.

$4(y + 1) = 0$ Since $4 \neq 0$, $(y + 1)$ must be 0.

$(x - 1)(x - 2) = 0$ implies that one of the factors is 0.

If $(x - 1) = 0$, solve for x: If $(x - 2) = 0$, solve for x:

$x - 1 + 1 = 0 + 1$ $x - 2 + 2 = 0 + 2$

$x = 1$ $x = 2$

Directions Find the value of the variable in each expression. Check your work.

1. $8y = 0$ _____   **6.** $2b^4 = 0$ _____

2. $4k = 0$ _____   **7.** $11x^2 = 0$ _____

3. $12p = 0$ _____   **8.** $7r^3 = 0$ _____

4. $32x = 0$ _____   **9.** $256n = 0$ _____

5. $10v = 0$ _____   **10.** $256n^3 = 0$ _____

Directions Solve these equations for the variable. Check your solutions.

11. $(13)(b + 5) = 0$ _____

12. $(n - 30)(6) = 0$ _____

13. $(a + 4)(a - 5) = 0$ _____

14. $(x + 4)(x + 7) = 0$ _____

15. $(x - 30)(x - 120) = 0$ _____

16. $(2d - 6)(5d + 5) = 0$ _____

17. $(2x - 1)(x + 2) = 0$ _____

18. $(x + 6)(x - 1) = 0$ _____

19. $(3y + 2)(y - 1) = 0$ _____

20. $(2k - 5)(3k + 6) = 0$ _____

Solving Quadratic Equations—Factoring

EXAMPLE   Solve $x^2 - 7x + 10 = 0$.

Step 1 Factor the equation. $x^2 - 7x + 10 = (x - 2)(x - 5) = 0$

Step 2 Set each factor equal to 0, and solve each factor for x.

$x - 2 = 0$ $x - 5 = 0$

$x = 2$ $x = 5$

Step 3 Check.

Let $x = 2$: $x^2 - 7x + 10 = (2)^2 - 7(2) + 10 = 4 - 14 + 10 = 0$ True

Let $x = 5$: $x^2 - 7x + 10 = (5)^2 - 7(5) + 10 = 25 - 35 + 10 = 0$ True

---

Directions   Find the solutions. Check your work.

1. $x^2 - 2x - 3 = 0$ _____

2. $b^2 + b - 12 = 0$ _____

3. $w^2 - 6w - 16 = 0$ _____

4. $2n^2 - n - 10 = 0$ _____

5. $x^2 - 4x - 21 = 0$ _____

6. $4a^2 + 5a - 6 = 0$ _____

7. $6x^2 - 7x - 3 = 0$ _____

8. $2n^2 + 5n - 3 = 0$ _____

9. $y^2 + 5y - 14 = 0$ _____

Directions   Solve the problem.

10. The square of a number d plus 5 times d plus 6 equals zero. Write an equation for this puzzle. Then factor the equation and solve for the factors to find the possible values of d.

_____

_____

_____

Organizing Data

A bar graph compares data by heights of bars. Study this bar graph.

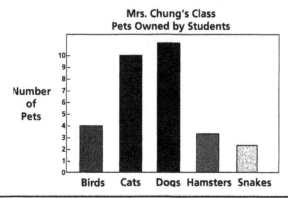

Directions Answer these questions about the bar graph in the example.

1. Which pet do the greatest number of Mrs. Chung's students own? _____

2. Which pet do the least number of Mrs. Chung's students own? _____

3. If the number scale on the left of the graph were covered up, would you still be able to answer questions 1 and 2? Explain.

    _____

4. How many birds do students in Mrs. Chung's class own? _____

5. How many hamsters do the students own? _____

6. If the number scale on the left of the graph were covered up, would you still be able to answer questions 4 and 5? Explain.

    _____

Directions Suppose 18 people are asked how much money they have in their pockets. Their answers are collected as data to fill the chart on the left. Use this data to complete the frequency table. One is done as an example for you.

How much money do you have in your pocket ? (in cents)		
18	5	30
75	25	95
25	25	120
16	90	65
38	35	75
28	39	42

Frequency Table		
Interval	Tally	Frequency
0–25¢	⊥⊥⊥⊥ I	6
26–50¢	**7.** _____	_____
51–75¢	**8.** _____	_____
76–100¢	**9.** _____	_____
101–125¢	**10.** _____	_____

Range, Mean, Median, and Mode

EXAMPLE Find range, mean, median, and mode of the following set of data:
{$3.98, $1.44, $3.15, $5.39, $1.44}.

   Range   Find the difference between the greatest and least values.
              $5.39 – $1.44 = $3.95 range

   Mean   Find the sum of the values. Then divide the sum by the
              number of data values (5).
              Sum = $15.40. $15.40 ÷ 5 = $3.08 mean

   Median   Arrange the data from least to greatest. Cross off greatest
              and least pairs until one value remains in the middle.
              That value is the median.

              ~~$1.44~~   ~~$1.44~~ $3.15   ~~$3.98~~   ~~$5.39~~

              $3.15 median

   Mode   Find any repeated values. They make up the mode.
              $1.44 mode

Directions Use a calculator to find the mean of each set of data.

  1. {17, 4, 29, 14}   _____

  2. {172, 51, 100, 87}   _____

  3. {4.5, 11.6, 8.8}   _____

  4. {553, 700, 297, 644, 199}   _____

  5. {600, 400, 100, 300, 500, 200} _____

  6. {18.1, 23.7, 10.5, 28.8, 21.4} _____

Directions Answer the questions to solve the problem.

Jenny collected data on the number of bulls-eyes she hit in archery practice
over a 7-day period. Here is her data set: {7, 4, 9, 12, 6, 19, 6}.

  7. Find the range of Jenny's data.   _____

  8. Find the arithmetic mean of the data. _____

  9. Find the median of the data.   _____

  10. Find the mode of the data.   _____

Box-and-Whiskers Plots

EXAMPLE The following data represents the number of strikes (knockouts of all bowling pins) the members of a bowling club bowled in their best game. Organize this data for a box-and-whiskers plot.

{11, 3, 4, 8, 6, 2, 9}

Step 1 Arrange the data from least to greatest. Label the lower extreme and upper extreme.

Step 2 Find and label the median of the data.

Step 3 Find the median of all the values below the median. Label this item the lower quartile.

Step 4 In a similar way, find and label the upper quartile.

2	3	4	6	8	9	11
↑	↑		↑		↑	↑
lower extreme	lower quartile		median		upper quartile	upper extreme

---

Directions For each data set, arrange the data from least to greatest value on the blank. Then answer the questions.

Data set: {$23.95, $8.15, $6.95, $14.69, $4.88, $24.20, $9.29, $13.12, $27.67, $10.99, $12.79}

_____

1. What is the median? _____

2. What is the lower extreme? _____

3. What is the upper extreme? _____

4. What is the lower quartile? _____

5. What is the upper quartile? _____

Data set: {66, 27, 15, 72, 21, 44, 39, 55, 48, 35, 19, 45, 40, 58, 30}

_____

6. What is the median? _____

7. What is the lower extreme? _____

8. What is the upper extreme? _____

9. What is the lower quartile? _____

10. What is the upper quartile? _____

The Probability Fraction

EXAMPLE The probability fraction: $\dfrac{\text{number of favorable outcomes}}{\text{number of possible outcomes}}$

A board game has a spinner with an arrow and 6 numbered regions. When the player spins the arrow, it lands on one of the six numbers (assume that it never stops on a line). Use the probability fraction to find the probability that the arrow will land on number 6.

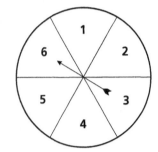

Step 1 Find the denominator.
The number of possible outcomes is 6 because there are 6 regions on the spinner.

Step 2 Find the numerator.
The number of favorable outcomes is 1 because the problem asks for number 6.

Step 3 Simplify the fraction if possible: $\frac{1}{6}$. No simplification is necessary.

The probability of spinning to number 6 is $\frac{1}{6}$.

Directions Use the probability fraction to solve these problems.

1. Suppose you drop a photograph on wet pavement. What is the probability that it will land image-side down on the pavement?   _____

2. Suppose a class of 24 has one student named Brad. Each day, the teacher lines up the students in random order. What is the probability on any day that Brad will be in front?   _____

3. In the same class, what is the probability on any day that Brad will be at the end of the line?   _____

4. In the same class, if Brad has a twin brother named Jackson, what is the probability that either twin will be at the front of the line?   _____

5. Suppose you come to a fork in the road and have no idea which fork to take. One fork leads directly to your destination, but the other leads away from it. What is the probability you will choose the correct fork?   _____

Probability and Complementary Events

EXAMPLE

- Suppose you toss a 1–6 number cube. It is *certain* that the outcome will be in the set {1, 2, 3, 4, 5, 6}.

- Suppose you toss a coin. It is *impossible* that the outcome will be both heads and tails.

- Suppose you close your eyes and point at random to a key on your computer keyboard. It is *likely* that you will point to a letter or number key.

- In the same situation, it is *not likely* that you will point to the letter *Q*.

Directions   Write one of the following words on the blank to describe the probability of each event: *certain, impossible, likely, not likely.*

1. With eyes closed, you pick a crayon at random from your box of 48 crayons. The color you pick is green. _____

2. The sun will come up tomorrow morning. _____

3. The first card you draw from a deck of regular playing cards is an ace. _____

4. Opening a book randomly, you open it to page 132. _____

5. Your book has 286 pages. You open the book randomly to page 400. _____

6. A pollster sends a questionnaire to 40 households in your community of 800 total households. One of these questionnaires arrives in your mailbox. _____

7. If you roll a 1–6 number cube, the number that rolls up will be the square of another integer. _____

8. If you roll a 1–6 number cube, the number that rolls up will be the square root of an integer. _____

9. The next person you pass on the sidewalk has a birthday in January. _____

10. You take one egg out of a dozen eggs in the refrigerator. It is *not* the last egg in the carton. _____

Tree Diagrams and Sample Spaces

EXAMPLE	A child is asked to select one crayon and one picture for coloring. Crayon choices are blue or red. The picture choices are a balloon or a star. What is the probability that the child will select *red* and a *star*?

Color choices: blue   red

Picture choices: balloon   star   balloon   star

The 4 possible choices: • blue and balloon   • red and balloon

• blue and star   • red and star

The probability is $\frac{1}{4}$: P (red, star) = $\frac{1}{4}$

Directions Suppose the child is still asked to choose between a blue or red crayon but is now offered 3 picture choices: balloon, star, or box. Use a tree diagram to determine the probability of each outcome.

1. Find P (red, box)   _____

2. Find P (red, star)   _____

3. Find P (blue, not star)   _____

4. Find P (blue, balloon)   _____

5. Find P (not blue, not balloon) _____

6. Find P (blue *or* red, box)   _____

7. Find P (red, *any* picture)   _____

8. Find P (*any* color, *any* picture) _____

Directions Solve the problems.

9. Suppose that runners may choose to run in the 5-km or 10-km race. What is the probability that the next runner to sign up will be female and will choose the 5-km race?   _____

10. For the same event, what is the probability that the next runner to sign up will be of either sex and will choose the 10-km race?   _____

Dependent and Independent Events

EXAMPLE   Suppose 2 children take one pencil each from the same box of 10 pencils. Half of the pencils have erasers, half do not. The first child chooses a pencil, then the second child chooses. What is the probability that both will choose a pencil with an eraser?

These events are dependent.

• The probability of an eraser for child A's choice is $\frac{5}{10}$, or $\frac{1}{2}$.

• The probability of an eraser for child B's choice is $\frac{5-1}{10-1}$, or $\frac{4}{9}$.

Suppose instead that each child chooses from an identical separate box of pencils. These events are independent, so each probability is identical.

Directions   Write whether the events are *dependent* or *independent*.

1. Each of 5 children chooses and keeps a marble from a bag of 5 marbles.   _____

2. A player in a board game rolls a number cube. Then a different player rolls the cube.   _____

3. A clothing store has one of a particular shirt left. One man buys the shirt. Then another man comes in, asking to buy the same shirt.   _____

4. Three children always sit on the backseat of their family car. Today, the first child sits in the middle. Then the second child sits down.   _____

5. One person draws a card from the deck, looks at it, and puts it back into the deck. The next person then draws from the deck.   _____

6. At the start of a board game, one person selects her playing piece from a bag of 7 pieces. Then you select your piece.   _____

7. A grab bag holds 3 wrapped gifts: one red, one blue, and one green. You take the gift wrapped in red. Then the person on your right takes one.   _____

8. A friend shows you a card trick, having you select 1 card out of 5. Then your friend repeats the same trick with someone else.   _____

9. Two trains are on the same track line. Train number one slows down. Train number two then slows down.   _____

10. A vase in a flower shop holds 3 flowers. After you take one, the florist replaces it. Then another person takes one.   _____

The Fundamental Principle of Counting

EXAMPLE

Find 4 factorial, or 4!

The factorial of 4 is the product of all positive integers from 4 down to 1.

Here is the calculation: $4 \cdot 3 \cdot 2 \cdot 1 = 24$

$4! = 24$

Directions Find the following factorials. You may use a calculator.

1. 8! _____

2. 11! _____

3. 9! _____

4. 5! _____

5. 7! _____

6. 3! _____

7. 6! _____

8. 10! _____

EXAMPLE How many different ways can Ben rearrange the letters in his name?

Possible letters in first position: 3

Possible letters in second position: $3 - 1 = 2$

Possible letters in third position: $2 - 1 = 1$

Ben can arrange the letters in his name $3 \cdot 2 \cdot 1 = 6$ ways.

You can also say that Ben can arrange the letters in 3! ways.

Directions Solve the problems.

9. How many different ways can Kristy rearrange the letters in her name? _____

10. The last 4 digits of Juan's phone number are 2138. In how many different ways can Juan rearrange these digits? _____

Choosing the Best Measure of Central Tendency

EXAMPLE

Some measures of central tendency more accurately describe a data set than others. Suppose four children and one grandparent are in a room. The ages of the children are 2, 4, 3, and 4 years old. The grandparent is 67 years old. Which measure(s) of central tendency best describes the ages of the people in the room?

Determine the mean, median, mode, and range of the ages. Then choose the best measure(s).

    mean = 16   median = 4   mode = 4   range = 65

If the mean were used to describe the ages of the people in the room, the impression would be given that the people in the room were teenagers, and this is not true. If the range were used to describe the ages of the people in the room, the impression would be given that the people in the room were much older than they actually are. Since most of the people in the room are very young, the median or the mode would provide the best description of the ages of the people in the room.

Directions Use the data in the table for Problems 1–5.

Time Spent Studying Last Night in minutes				
30	10	45	0	80
0	40	60	10	5

1. Find the mean of the data.   _____

2. Find the median of the data.   _____

3. Find the mode of the data.   _____

4. Find the range of the data.   _____

5. Which measure(s) best describes the length of time the students shown in the table studied last night? Explain.

_____

_____

_____

Fractions as Rational Numbers

EXAMPLE

Write $\frac{6}{18}$ in simplest form.

Step 1 Prime factorization of 6 and 18:

$$\frac{6}{18} = \frac{2 \cdot 3}{2 \cdot 3 \cdot 3}$$

Step 2 Identify common prime factors and calculate the GCF.
- Common prime factors = 2 • 3
- GCF = 2 • 3 = 6

Step 3 Divide the fraction numerator and denominator by the GCF, 6.

$$\frac{6}{18} \div \frac{6}{6} = \frac{1}{3}$$

Step 4 Check. $\frac{6}{18} = \frac{1}{3}$, so 6 • 3 = 18 • 1, and 18 = 18.

Directions Write each fraction in simplest form. Check your work.

1. $\frac{8}{64}$ _____

2. $\frac{13}{52}$ _____

3. $\frac{12}{39}$ _____

4. $\frac{30}{48}$ _____

5. $\frac{34}{51}$ _____

6. $\frac{3}{63}$ _____

7. $\frac{21}{28}$ _____

8. $\frac{16}{-48}$ _____

9. $\frac{35}{60}$ _____

10. $\frac{19}{57}$ _____

11. $\frac{11}{-88}$ _____

12. $\frac{354}{600}$ _____

Directions Solve the problems.

13. Jamille found that 3 members of her class of 27 are younger than she, so she exclaimed, "$\frac{3}{27}$ of the class is younger than I am." How could Jamille have simplified her statement mathematically?

_____

14. A baker bakes 48 dozen doughnuts each morning. She sells 18 dozen in her store and fills orders with the rest. Write a fraction to show the portion of doughnuts the baker sells in her store. Simplify your answer. _____

15. Nick observed that he had finished 15 out of 36 homework problems, or $\frac{15}{36}$ of the total. Simplify Nick's fraction. _____

Algebraic Fractions—Rational Expressions

EXAMPLE

Simplify $\dfrac{6n^2}{9n^3}$

Step 1 Find the GCF of numerator and denominator.

$$\frac{6n^2}{9n^3} = \frac{2 \cdot 3 \cdot n \cdot n}{3 \cdot 3 \cdot n \cdot n \cdot n}$$

The GCF is $3 \cdot n \cdot n$ or $3n^2$

Step 2 Divide both the numerator and denominator by the GCF.

$$\frac{6n^2}{9n^3} \div \frac{3n^2}{3n^2} = \frac{2}{3n}$$

Step 3 Check. $\dfrac{6n^2}{9n^3} = \dfrac{2}{3n}$ $18n^3 = 18n^3$ True

---

Directions Simplify these expressions. Check your work.

1. $\dfrac{c^2}{c^4}$ _____

2. $\dfrac{15x}{27x^3}$ _____

3. $\dfrac{m^4}{m^9}$ _____

4. $\dfrac{7c^3d^2}{21c^5d^3}$ _____

5. $\dfrac{18ab^2}{24a^3b^2}$ _____

6. $\dfrac{7w^2yz^3}{11w^3y^4z^8}$ _____

7. $\dfrac{y(x+3)}{y^2(x+8)}$ _____

8. $\dfrac{(x+2)}{(x+2)^2}$ _____

9. $\dfrac{y-9}{y^2-11y+18}$ _____

10. $\dfrac{5(x+1)}{x^2+4x+3}$ _____

11. $\dfrac{r+10}{r^2-100}$ _____

12. $\dfrac{a+4}{a^2+8a+16}$ _____

13. $\dfrac{b^3(k-33)}{b^3(k+14)}$ _____

14. $\dfrac{x-5}{x^2-25}$ _____

15. $\dfrac{4y^2(z+1)}{4y^3(z-1)}$ _____

16. $\dfrac{w-3}{w^2-6w+9}$ _____

17. $\dfrac{b^2-9}{(b+3)(b-3)}$ _____

18. $\dfrac{-k^2+49}{(k-7)(5k^5+7)}$ _____

Directions Solve the problems.

19. The storage area of warehouse A is $x^2 - y^2$ square m. The storage area of warehouse B is $x + y$ square m. The expression $\dfrac{x+y}{x^2-y^2}$ square m shows the relationship between these two areas in fraction form. Is the fraction in its simplest form? If not, simplify. _____

20. Factory A packages $4x^2$ pencils a day. Factory B packages $6x^3$ pencils a day. The expression $\dfrac{4x^2}{6x^3}$ shows the relationship between the output of the two factories. Simplify the expression. _____

Multiplying and Dividing Algebraic Fractions

EXAMPLE Find the quotient of $\frac{4}{5} \div \frac{2}{3}$.

Step 1 Multiply by the reciprocal.

$\frac{4}{5} \cdot \frac{3}{2} = \frac{12}{10}$

Step 2 Simplify.

$\frac{12}{10} = \frac{6}{5}$ $\frac{6}{5} = \frac{5}{5} + \frac{1}{5} = 1 + \frac{1}{5} = 1\frac{1}{5}$

Step 3 Check.

$\frac{6}{5} \cdot \frac{2}{3} = \frac{12}{15} = \frac{4}{5}$ True

---

Directions Find and check each quotient. Simplify your answer whenever possible.

1. $\frac{1}{7} \div \frac{1}{2}$ _____

2. $\frac{3}{10} \div \frac{2}{5}$ _____

3. $2\frac{1}{2} \div \frac{1}{3}$ _____

4. $1\frac{8}{9} \div \frac{1}{2}$ _____

5. $1\frac{2}{3} \div 1\frac{1}{2}$ _____

6. $\frac{1}{k} \div \frac{4}{5}$ _____

7. $\frac{c}{d^2} \div \frac{d^3}{c^2}$ _____

8. $\frac{3}{2w^2} \div 1\frac{1}{3}$ _____

9. $\frac{11}{4x^2y^3} \div \frac{1}{4}$ _____

10. $\frac{n^2}{2} \div \frac{3}{10}$ _____

11. $\frac{n}{m^2} \div \frac{n^2}{m}$ _____

12. $\frac{5ab}{cd} \div 2\frac{1}{7}$ _____

13. $\frac{b^3}{2c^3} \div \frac{1}{5}$ _____

14. $\frac{3}{ab^2} \div \frac{x}{ab^2}$ _____

15. $\frac{x+1}{x^2y^2} \div \frac{x^2-1}{x^2y^2}$ _____

16. $\frac{1}{w^2-9} \div \frac{w+3}{w-3}$ _____

Directions Answer the questions to solve the problem.

In math class, Raphael learned that dividing by a number is the same as multiplying by its reciprocal. "Four is really $\frac{4}{1}$," said Raphael. "So dividing by 4 is the same as multiplying by $\frac{1}{4}$." Use Raphael's idea about reciprocals to complete the blanks.

17. Dividing by 8 is the same as multiplying by _____.

18. Dividing by _____ is the same as multiplying by $\frac{1}{10}$.

19. Dividing by 22 is the same as multiplying by _____.

20. Dividing by _____ is the same as multiplying by $\frac{1}{7}$.

Complex Fractions and the LCM

EXAMPLE   Simplify $\dfrac{\frac{2}{3}}{\frac{1}{2}}$

Step 1 Find the LCM of each denominator.
Multiples of 3: 3, 6, 9, 12 …
Multiples of 2: 2, 4, 6, 8 …
The LCM = 6.

Step 2 Multiply by the LCM and simplify. $\dfrac{\frac{2}{3}}{\frac{1}{2}} \cdot \dfrac{\frac{6}{1}}{\frac{6}{1}} = \dfrac{\frac{12}{3}}{\frac{6}{2}}$

$= \dfrac{4}{3}$ or $1\dfrac{1}{3}$

Directions Find the LCM for each pair.

1. 2, 3 _____

2. 6, 7 _____

3. 15, 6 _____

4. 11, 4 _____

5. 9, 10 _____

6. 3, 17 _____

7. 6, 24 _____

8. 8, 32 _____

9. 7, 22 _____

10. 9, 15 _____

11. $12x, 5x$ _____

12. $3a, 7a$ _____

13. $5b, 8b$ _____

14. $k, 12k$ _____

15. $2n, 13n$ _____

16. $4k, 7k$ _____

Directions Simplify each complex fraction.

17. $\dfrac{\frac{2}{3}}{\frac{2}{3}}$ _____

18. $\dfrac{\frac{1}{2}}{\frac{2}{3}}$ _____

19. $\dfrac{\frac{7}{8}}{\frac{3}{4}}$ _____

20. $\dfrac{\frac{3}{4}}{\frac{7}{8}}$ _____

21. $\dfrac{\frac{9}{10}}{\frac{3}{4}}$ _____

22. $\dfrac{\frac{1}{6x}}{\frac{1}{7x}}$ _____

23. $\dfrac{\frac{3n}{16}}{\frac{1}{4}}$ _____

24. $\dfrac{\frac{8}{25w}}{\frac{3}{5w}}$ _____

25. $\dfrac{\frac{1}{8a}}{\frac{2}{9}}$ _____

Least Common Multiples and Prime Factors

EXAMPLE Find the LCM of 12 and 10.

Step 1 List prime factors of the denominators, 12 and 10.

$12 = 2 \cdot 2 \cdot 3$ $10 = 2 \cdot 5$

Step 2 Count prime factors:

• greatest number of times 2 appears: twice (2 • 2)

• greatest number of times 3 appears: once (3)

• greatest number of times 5 appears: once (5)

Step 3 Find the product of the above:

$2 \cdot 2 \cdot 3 \cdot 5 = 60 =$ LCM of 12 and 10

Directions Using prime factorization, find the least common multiple for each pair.

1. 3, 8   _____

2. 15, 25   _____

3. 14, 38   _____

4. 6, 14   _____

5. 16, 10   _____

6. 5, 7   _____

7. x^4y, xy^2 _____

8. cd^4, c^2d^3 _____

Directions Solve the problems.

9. A store display has 2 blinking lights. One blinks every 15 seconds and the other blanks every 12 seconds. After how many seconds will the lights blink at the same instant? (Hint: find the LCM of the numbers.)

_____

10. Geri has play blocks that are 4 inches tall. Bette has blocks that are 6 inches tall. Suppose the two tots each stack their own blocks into towers, side by side. What is the *least* height at which both towers can be the same height?

_____

Sums and Differences

EXAMPLE   Find the sum of $\frac{2}{9} + \frac{2}{15}$.

Step 1 Find the LCM of the denominators, 9 and 15.

$9 = 3 \cdot 3 \qquad 15 = 3 \cdot 5$

The LCM of 9 and 15 is $3 \cdot 3 \cdot 5 = 45$.

Step 2 Multiply each fraction by 1 in a form that will make the denominator 45.

$\frac{2}{9} \cdot \frac{5}{5} = \frac{10}{45}$

$\frac{2}{15} \cdot \frac{3}{3} = \frac{6}{45}$

Step 3 Add the fractions and simplify.

$\frac{10}{45} + \frac{6}{45} = \frac{16}{45}$

$\frac{16}{45}$ cannot be further simplified.

Directions Find the LCM, then add or subtract. Write your answer in simplest form.

1. $\frac{4}{7} + \frac{3}{5}$ _____

2. $\frac{5}{14} + \frac{2}{21}$ _____

3. $\frac{8n}{15} - \frac{5n}{12}$ _____

4. $\frac{21y}{14} - \frac{5y}{21}$ _____

5. $\frac{w}{2} - \frac{w}{5}$ _____

6. $\frac{2}{c} - \frac{3c}{1}$ _____

7. $\frac{1}{n} + \frac{n}{m}$ _____

8. $\frac{k}{k+1} - \frac{3}{k}$ _____

Directions Solve the problems.

9. Estelle estimated that she mowed $\frac{2}{5}$ of the yard on Friday. Then she estimated that her brother Juaquin mowed another $\frac{1}{7}$ the next day. Together, what portion of the yard had they mowed? _____

10. Roger figured that he had done $\frac{17}{20}$ of his homework. His friend Mike said he had done $\frac{3}{8}$ of his homework. What is the difference between the amount of homework Roger and Mike had completed? _____

Proportions and Fractions in Equations

EXAMPLE   Solve $\frac{4}{x} = \frac{2}{16}$.

Step 1 Set up the cross products.

$(4)(16) = (x)(2)$

$2x = (4)(16)$ Commutative Property

Step 2 Solve for x.

$(\frac{1}{2})(2x) = (4)(16)(\frac{1}{2})$

$x = 32$

Step 3 Check. $\frac{4}{32} = \frac{2}{16}$

$(2)(32) = (4)(16)$

$64 = 64$ True

Directions Solve for the variable. Check your work.

1. $\frac{a}{18} = \frac{2}{3}$ _____

2. $\frac{9}{x} = \frac{3}{5}$ _____

3. $\frac{k}{-12} = \frac{-3}{4}$ _____

4. $\frac{2}{7} = \frac{y}{-35}$ _____

5. $\frac{3}{4} = \frac{5}{x}$ _____

6. $\frac{3}{n} = \frac{4}{n-2}$ _____

7. $\frac{6}{r-2} = -3$ _____

8. $\frac{3(w+5)}{2} = \frac{5(w-2)}{3}$ _____

Directions Solve the problems.

9. A slaw recipe for 12 servings uses 6 cups of chopped cabbage. How much cabbage will be needed for 28 servings?

_____

10. A farmer uses $1\frac{1}{3}$ bushels of wheat seed to plant 2 acres of wheat. How much will he need to plant 14 acres? (Hint: change $1\frac{1}{3}$ to an improper fraction first.)

_____

More Solutions to Equations with Fractions

EXAMPLE Solve $\frac{1}{5}x = 3$ using multiplication and using division.

Multiplication	**Division**
$(\frac{1}{5})x = 3$	$(\frac{1}{5})x = 3$
$(5)(\frac{1}{5})x = (3)(5)$	$\dfrac{\frac{1}{5}x}{\frac{1}{5}} = \dfrac{3}{\frac{1}{5}}$
$x = 15$	$x = 3(\frac{5}{1}) = 15$

Check solution.

$\frac{1}{5}(15) = 3$

$3 = 3$ True

Directions Solve using division or multiplication. Check your answers.

1. $\frac{2}{3}b = 6$ _____

2. $\frac{3}{7}k = 9$ _____

3. $\frac{2}{11}a = 4$ _____

4. $\frac{5}{8}m - \frac{1}{2} = -2$ _____

5. $\frac{1}{2}x + 4 = 9$ _____

6. $\frac{2}{3}p - \frac{1}{2} = 4$ _____

7. $\frac{1}{3}a + 1 = 14$ _____

8. $\frac{1}{5}y + 12 = 17$ _____

Directions Solve the problems.

9. Danny subtracted the fraction $\frac{1}{8}$ from $\frac{1}{3}$ of a certain number to get a result of 1. What was the number?

_____

10. Tim scored 2,200 on a video game, or $\frac{8}{9}$ of the total points that Dru scored. How many points did Dru score?

_____

The Greatest Common Factor of Large Numbers

EXAMPLE

Using prime factorization to find the GCF of two whole numbers is difficult when the whole numbers are large. To find the GCF of two large whole numbers, use the following theorem.

If x and y are two whole numbers and $x \geq y$, then $GCF(x,y) = GCF(x - y, y)$.

Find GCF(403, 78)

Apply the theorem repeatedly.

GCF(403, 78)=   GCF(403 − 78, 78) = GCF(325, 78)

                    GCF(325 − 78, 78) = GCF(247, 78)

                    GCF(247 − 78, 78) = GCF(169, 78)

                    GCF(169 − 78, 78) = GCF(91, 78)

                    GCF(91 − 78, 78) = GCF(13, 78)

                              ↑   The GCF of 403 and 78 is 13.

Directions   Use the theorem shown above to find the GCF of each pair of whole numbers.

1. (323, 153)   _____

2. (135, 54)   _____

3. (324, 72)   _____

4. (189, 45)   _____

5. (312, 96)   _____

6. (630, 180)   _____

7. (648, 144)   _____

8. (954, 424)   _____

9. (1,440, 288)   _____

10. (15,015, 1,365) _____

Denominators and Zero

EXAMPLE   For what value(s) of n is $\frac{3}{n-4}$ undefined?

If $(n-4)=0$, the fraction is undefined. Solving the equation:

$$n-4=0$$
$$n-4+4=0+4$$
$$n=4$$

Therefore, the fraction is undefined if $n=4$.

Directions   Determine the value(s) for which each expression is undefined.

1. $\frac{1}{d-3}$ _____

2. $\frac{2}{a+5}$ _____

3. $\frac{7}{w-9}$ _____

4. $\frac{1}{5x}$ _____

5. $\frac{2}{9y}$ _____

6. $\frac{5b}{b^2-16}$ _____

7. $\frac{1}{x^2-25}$ _____

8. $\frac{15k^2}{45k^3}$ _____

9. $\frac{1}{x^2-9x+14}$ _____

10. $\frac{3a}{-7a}$ _____

11. $\frac{4x}{\frac{1}{2}x}$ _____

12. $\frac{10}{y+5}$ _____

13. $\frac{10}{\frac{3}{4}y}$ _____

14. $\frac{12x^2}{48x^3}$ _____

15. $\frac{2}{\frac{3}{7k}}$ _____

16. $\frac{2c}{c^2-36}$ _____

17. $\frac{5b}{-19b}$ _____

18. $\frac{x+2}{x^2-3x-10}$ _____

19. $\frac{17}{17x}$ _____

20. $\frac{15}{x-15}$ _____

The Coordinate System

EXAMPLE   Graph (2, 3).

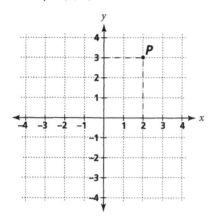

Point *P* is located at (2, 3).

Directions   Write the ordered pair that represents the location of each point on the graph.

1. Point *W*   _____

2. Point *K*   _____

3. Point *R*   _____

4. Point *G*   _____

5. Point *T*   _____

6. Point *A*   _____

7. Point *N*   _____

8. Point *D*   _____

9. Point *Q*   _____

10. Point *B*   _____

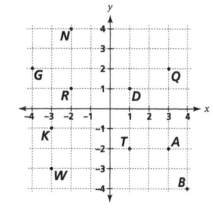

 Algebra

Graphing Equations

EXAMPLE   Graph $y = 3x$.

Step 1   Assign values to x. Let $x = -1$ and $x = 1$.

Step 2   Solve for y in $y = 3x$.

$y = 3(-1)$ $y = 3(1)$

$y = -3$ $y = 3$

So $(-1, -3)$ So $(1, 3)$

Step 3   Plot the points $(-1, -3)$ and $(1, 3)$.

Then graph and label the line.

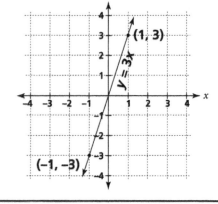

Directions   Solve each equation for y when the value of x is given.

1. $y = 4x - 6$; $x = 1$ _____

2. $y = 3x - 3$; $x = 1$ _____

3. $y = 2x - 4$; $x = 2$ _____

4. $y = 4x - 2$; $x = -1$ _____

Directions   Given the x-values, solve for y. Then graph the equation and label the line.

5. $y = 2x + 1$

$x = -1$ _____

$x = 1$ _____

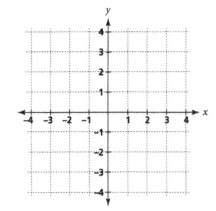

Intercepts of Lines

EXAMPLE   Find the following *x*- and *y*-intercepts.

- Find the *y*-intercept of $y = 2x - 2$.

  Substitute $x = 0$ into the equation. Solve for *y*.

  $y = 2(0) - 2$

  $y = -2$ This is the *y*-intercept.

- Find the *x*-intercept of $y = 3x + 1$.

  Substitute $y = 0$ into the equation. Solve for *x*.

  $0 = 3x + 1$

  $x = \frac{1}{-3}$ This is the *x*-intercept.

Directions   Find the *x*-intercept and *y*-intercept of each graph.

$y = 2x + 3$

1. *x*-intercept _____

2. *y*-intercept _____

$y = 3x - 4$

3. *x*-intercept _____

4. *y*-intercept _____

$y = -2x + 2$

5. *x*-intercept _____

6. *y*-intercept _____

$y = 2x + 7$

7. *x*-intercept _____

8. *y*-intercept _____

$y = -x + 3$

9. *x*-intercept _____

10. *y*-intercept _____

Slopes of Lines

EXAMPLE   Find the slope of a line that passes through (–3, –2) and (2, 4).

Step 1 Label one ordered pair (x_1, y_1) and the other (x_2, y_2).

$(x_1 = -3, y_1 = -2)$ $(x_2 = 2, y_2 = 4)$

Step 2 Substitute in the slope formula and solve.

$$m = \frac{y_2 - y_1}{x_2 - x_1}$$

$$= \frac{4 - (-2)}{2 - (-3)} = \frac{6}{5} \text{ or } 1\frac{1}{5}$$

Directions Find the slope of a line that passes through the following points.

1. (1, 3) (2, 4) _____   **5.** (6, –2) (–3, 4) _____

2. (–3, 1) (3, 13) _____   **6.** (6, 4) (2, 1) _____

3. (1, 3) (5, 6) _____   **7.** (–3, 2) (–1, –1) _____

4. (2, 5) (3, 4) _____   **8.** (0, 1) (5, –2) _____

EXAMPLE

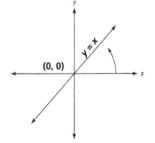

Positive Slope

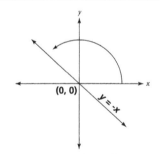

Negative Slope

Directions Solve the problems. Refer to the graphs of slopes shown.

9. Think of a clock as a graph with the pivot of its hands at (0, 0). When the time is 10:20, the hands form a straight line. Does this line have positive or negative slope?

_____

10. When the time is 8:10, is the slope of the line the hands form negative or positive?

_____

Writing Linear Equations

EXAMPLE   Write the equation of a line that passes through (6, 1) and (3, –2).

Step 1 Find the slope, m.

$$m = \frac{y_2 - y_1}{x_2 - x_1}$$

$$= \frac{-2 - 1}{3 - 6} = \frac{-3}{-3} = 1$$

Step 2 Find the y-intercept, using known point (6, 1).

$$y = mx + b \qquad 1 = 1(6) + b \qquad b = -5$$

Step 3 Substitute slope and y-intercept in $y = mx + b$:

$$y = (1)x + (-5) \text{ or } y = x - 5$$

Directions   Write the equation of the line that passes through each pair of points.

1. $(6, 0)\ (0, 2)$ _____

2. $(-2, 0)\ (-1, -3)$ _____

3. $(1, 2)\ (5, 8)$ _____

4. $(6, 6)\ (3, 2)$ _____

5. $(0, 4)\ (-2, 0)$ _____

6. $(-2, 3)(1, 5)$ _____

7. $(-2, 7)\ (2, 1)$ _____

8. $(6, 6)\ (8, 3)$ _____

Directions   Graph the line that passes through the following points. Then find the equation of the line and label it on the graph.

9. $(2, 1)\ (-2, -2)$

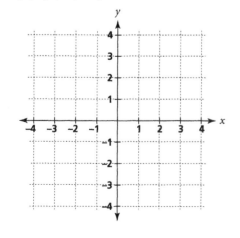

10. $(-4, 4)\ (2, 0)$

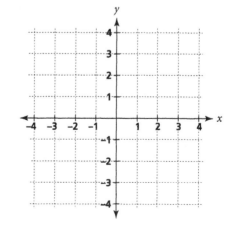

Lines as Functions

A function is a rule that associates every *x*-value with one and only one *y*-value. If a vertical line crosses a graph more than once, the graph is *not* a function.

- A *circle* is *not* a function. A vertical line will cross it at two points.

- A *straight line* is a function. A vertical line crosses it at one point only.

Directions Is each graph an example of a function? Write *yes* or *no*. Explain your answer.

1. _____
_____
_____

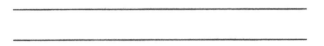

2. _____
_____
_____

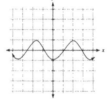

3. _____
_____
_____

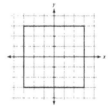

4. _____
_____
_____

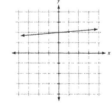

5. _____
_____
_____

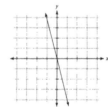

Domain and Range of a Function

EXAMPLE Find the range of the function $y = f(x) = 3x + 1$ for the domain –2, 0, 3, 6
Substitute the domain values in $f(x)$

$x = -2$ $y = f(-2) = 3(-2) + 1 = -5$ so $y = -5$	$x = 3$ $y = f(3) = 3(3) + 1 = 10$ so $y = 10$
$x = 0$ $y = f(0) = 3(0) + 1 = 1$ so $y = 1$	$x = 6$ $y = f(6) = 3(5) + 1 = 16$ so $y = 16$

EXAMPLE Determine the domain and the range of a function from a graphed line and its end points.

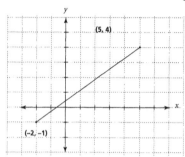

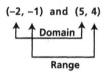

Domain = $-2 \le x \le 5$
Range = $-1 \le y \le 4$

Directions Determine the range for each function with the given domain.

1. $f(x) = 2x + 5$ domain: $-1, 0, 3, 7, 10$ range: _____

4. $f(x) = x^2 + 3x - 4$ domain: $-3, 0, 2, 4, 6$ range: _____

2. $f(x) = x^3$ domain: $-1, 0, 2, 5, 8$ range: _____

5. $f(x) = 3x - 9$ domain: $-4, -3, 0, 1, 8$ range: _____

3. $f(x) = \frac{1}{2}x - 2$ domain: $\frac{-1}{2}, 0, 3, 5, 9$ range: _____

6. $f(x) = x^2 - x$ domain: $-3, -1, 0, 2, 3$ range: _____

Directions Determine the domain and the range from the graph and the given ordered pairs.

7. domain: _____ range: _____

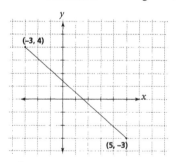

8. domain: _____ range: _____

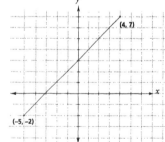

9. domain: _____ range: _____

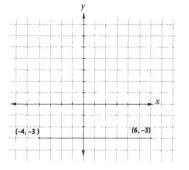

10. domain: _____ range: _____

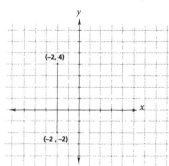

Graphing Inequalities: $y < mx + b$, $y > mx + b$

EXAMPLE

Graph the region represented by $y > x + 4$.

Step 1 Use $y = x + 4$ and substitution to find two points on the line. Let $x = 0$, and then let $x = -1$. The two points are $(0, 4)$ and $(-1, 3)$.

Step 2 Plot the two points and connect them with a broken line.

Step 3 Shade the region *above* the line. Label it $y > x + 4$.

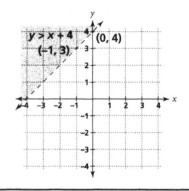

Directions Graph the region represented by each line.

1. $y > 2x - 1$

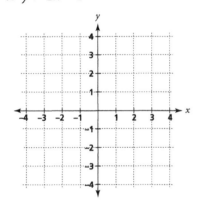

2. $y < x + 2$

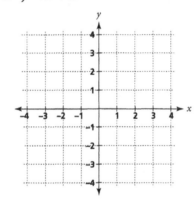

3. $y > -x + 3$

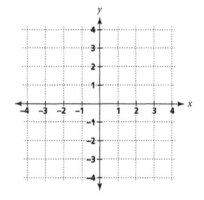

Directions Write an inequality to label the shaded region in each graph.

4. _____

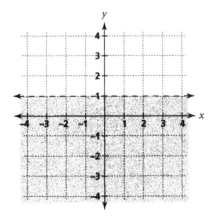

5. _____

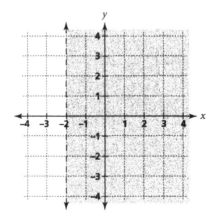

Graphing Inequalities: $y \leq mx + b$, $y \geq mx + b$

EXAMPLE
  The two graphs show the inequalities $y \geq 3x - 1$ and $y > 3x - 1$.
Can you see a difference between these graphs?

The only difference between the two graphs is that the line of the equation $y \geq 3x - 1$ is a solid, unbroken line. This solid line indicates that the points on the line of the equation are also included in the graph of the inequality.

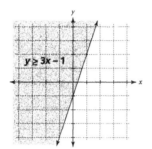
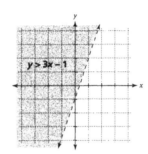

Directions   Write the inequality that describes the shaded region.

1. _____

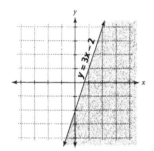

2. _____

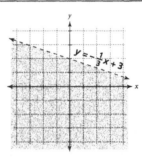

3. _____

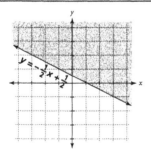

4. _____

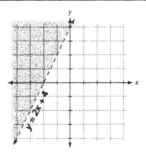

Directions   Answer the question.

5. Suppose you were to graph the inequalities $y \leq 2x$ and $y < 2x$. What would be the difference between the two graphs?

Graphs Without Numbers

EXAMPLE

Every graph is a picture of something that has happened sometime in the past or is happening now. You can often determine what a graph is about just by its general shape. The first item below is done for you. It shows how to read the shape of a graph.

Directions Match each written description with a graph. Write the letter of the graph on the blank.

Speeding baseball being caught by an outfielder   **D**

A.

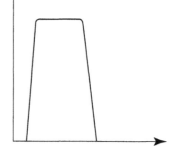

1. Helicopter rising, moving off in a direction for a while, then lowering   _____

2. Helicopter rising, hovering briefly, then descending   _____

3. Wave motion such as an ocean wave or sound wave   _____

B.

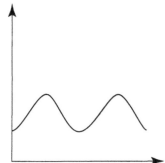

C.

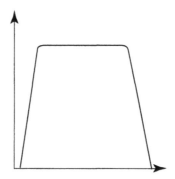

D.

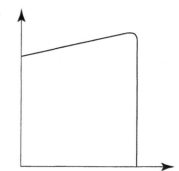

Directions Answer the questions.

4. On all the graphs that appear on this page, what is the understood point of origin? _____

5. Why do you think it may be convenient in many situations to use a graph with only positive points?

_____

_____

_____

Parallel Lines

EXAMPLE

Lines having the same slope are parallel. In an equation of the form $y = mx + b$, coefficient m of the variable x gives the slope. For example, in $y = 3x + 4$, the slope is 3.

A line for an equation in the form $y = $ constant is a horizontal line.

A line for an equation in the form $x = $ constant is a vertical line.

Study the example lines in the graph.

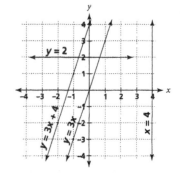

Directions Write the equation of the line parallel to the given line and passing through the given point, which is the y-intercept.

1. $y = x + 7$; $(0, 4)$ _____

2. $y = 2x - 2$; $(0, 2)$ _____

3. $y = 4x + 1$; $(0, -4)$ _____

4. $y = 2x + 3$; $(0, 5)$ _____

5. $y = 3x + 3$; $(0, -3)$ _____

6. $y = 4x - 2$; $(0, -1)$ _____

7. $y = x - 3$; $(0, 1)$ _____

8. $y = 5x - 1$; $(0, 1)$ _____

Directions Solve the problems.

9. If you plotted the following equations on a single graph, which line would stand out? Write the letter of the answer and explain.

_____

_____

a. $x = -7$ **d.** $y = 3$ **g.** $x = -8$

b. $y = -6$ **e.** $x = 4$ **h.** $y = 2x + 4$

c. $x = 3$ **f.** $y = 9$ **i.** $y = 2$

10. Will graphs for these equations show parallel lines? Explain.

$$y = 6x + 1 \qquad y = 6x - 5$$

_____

_____

Describing Parallel Lines

EXAMPLE   Write the equation of a line that is parallel to the line $y = 2x + 3$ and passes through the point $(-2, 1)$.

Step 1 The slope is 2, so $y = 2x + b$.

Step 2 Substitute the values from the point $(-2, 1)$ and solve for b.

$$y = 2x + b$$
$$1 = 2(-2) + b$$
$$b = 5$$

Step 3 Substitute this value for b in the equation.

$$y = 2x + 5$$

Directions Write the equation of the line parallel to the given line and passing through the given point.

1. $y = x + 4$; $(2, 5)$ _____

2. $y = 3x - 1$; $(1, 4)$ _____

3. $y = 2x - 2$; $(2, 8)$ _____

4. $y = x - 7$; $(4, 6)$ _____

5. $y = 3x - 3$; $(-2, -5)$ _____

Directions Rewrite each equation in the form $y = mx + b$. Then write an equation for a line parallel to the first and passing through the given point.

6. $6y = 3x - 12$; $(2, -4)$ _____

7. $\frac{1}{2}y = 3x$; $(-2, -9)$ _____

8. $5y = 4x + 5$; $(-5, -4)$ _____

9. $10y = -20x - 20$; $(1, -3)$ _____

10. $3x = 3y - 12$; $(-5, -11)$ _____

Intersecting Lines—Common Solutions

EXAMPLE   Look at these examples of graphed equations.

A. 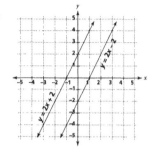   **B.**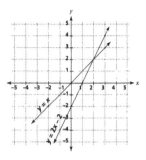

- Equations having the same slope are represented by parallel lines that do not intersect. In Example A, $y = 2x + 2$ and $y = 2x - 2$ have the same slope, 2.

- Equations having unlike slope are represented by lines that *do* intersect. In Example B, $y = x$ has slope of 1 and $y = 2x - 2$ has slope of 2.

Directions   Do these systems of equations have a common solution? Tell why or why not.

1. $y = 2x + 3$

    $y = 2x - 1$

2. $y = 3x - 4$

    $y = -3x + 1$

3. $y = \frac{2}{3}x + 2$

    $y = \frac{3}{2}x + 2$

_____

_____

_____

Directions   Answer the questions to solve the problem. Explain your answer.

A large state in a desert country consists of flat land with few towns. The state has a rectangular shape, and the major roads are straight lines. Engineers use a grid map with x-axis and y-axis to design roads in this desert state. They describe road positions by equations, as follows:

Road A-1: $y = 3x + 5$ **Road A-2:** $y = x - 2$ **Road B-1:** $y = 3x - 1$

4. Will roads A-1 and B-1 ever intersect?

_____

5. Will roads A-1 and A-2 ever intersect?

_____

Solving Linear Equations—Substitution

EXAMPLE

Find the common solution for the system:

$y = -2x + 4$ $y = -x + 1$

Step 1 From the second equation, substitute the value of y into the first equation.

$-x + 1 = -2x + 4$

Step 2 Solve for x.

$x = 3$

Step 3 Substitute this value of x into the first equation to solve for y.

$y = -2x + 4$

$y = -2(3) + 4$

$y = -2$ The common solution is the ordered pair (3, -2).

Step 4 Check. Substitute the x and y values in each equation.

$y = -2x + 4$ $y = -x + 1$

$-2 = -2(3) + 4$ $-2 = -(3) + 1$

$-2 = -2$ True $-2 = -2$ True

Directions Find the common solution for each system of equations.
Check each solution.

1. $2x + y = 4$ $2x + 3y = 0$ _____

2. $2x + y = 0$ $x - y = 1$ _____

3. $3x + 4y = -11$ $7x - 5y = 3$ _____

4. $2x + y = -1$ $-2x + y = 3$ _____

5. $3x - 5y = 4$ $4x + 3y = 15$ _____

6. $3x - 2y = 5$ $-4x + 3y = 1$ _____

7. $3x - 4y = 5$ $5x + 4y = 3$ _____

8. $4x = 3y - 10$ $2y = 22 - 5x$ _____

9. $2x + 6y = 14$ $3x - 4y = -5$ _____

10. $\frac{1}{2}y = 2 - 2x$ $6x = y + 1$ _____

Solving Linear Equations—Elimination

EXAMPLE Find the common solution for the system:

$$x + y = 3 \qquad 3x - y = 1$$

Step 1 Add the equations to eliminate the y-term.

$$x + y = 3$$
$$3x - y = 1$$
$$4x \quad = 4 \qquad \text{so } x = 1$$

Step 2 Substitute the value of x into either equation.

$$1 + y = 3$$
$$y = 2 \qquad \text{The common solution is } (1, 2).$$

Step 3 Check. Substitute for x and y in each equation.

$$x + y = 3 \qquad\qquad 3x - y = 1$$
$$1 + 2 = 3 \qquad\qquad 3(1) - 2 = 1$$
$$3 = 3 \quad \text{True} \qquad 1 = 1 \quad \text{True}$$

Directions Find the common solution for each system of equations using elimination and/or substitution.

1. $x + y = 20$ $\qquad$ $x - y = 10$ $\qquad$ _____

2. $x + y = 8$ $\qquad$ $x - y = -2$ $\qquad$ _____

3. $x + y = 5$ $\qquad$ $x - y = -3$ $\qquad$ _____

4. $x - y = 4$ $\qquad$ $3x + 2y = 7$ $\qquad$ _____

5. $5x + 5y = -5$ $\qquad$ $3x - y = -7$ $\qquad$ _____

6. $4x - y = 1$ $\qquad$ $2x + y = 17$ $\qquad$ _____

7. $2x - y = 4$ $\qquad$ $2x + 4y = 4$ $\qquad$ _____

8. $-x + 3y = 14$ $\qquad$ $x + 22 = 5y$ $\qquad$ _____

9. $8x - 6y = 2$ $\qquad$ $2x + 3y = 2$ $\qquad$ _____

10. $2x - 5y = 10$ $\qquad$ $3x - 2y = -7$ $\qquad$ _____

Graphing Systems of Linear Equations

EXAMPLE

Use a graph to find the common solution for these equations:

$x + y = 3$ $\qquad\qquad$ $3x - y = 1$

Step 1 Find the x- and y-intercepts for each equation.

$x + y = 3$	$3x - y = 1$
$0 + y = 3$, so $y = 3$	$3(0) - y = 1$, so $y = -1$
$x + 0 = 3$, so $x = 3$	$3x - 0 = 1$, so $x = \frac{1}{3}$
x-int. = 3, y-int. = 3	x-int. = $\frac{1}{3}$, y-int. = -1

Step 2 Plot the intercepts for each equation (2 points). Draw the line connecting them. Read the point of intersection from the graph: (1, 2).

Step 3 Check by substituting the solution in the equations.

Directions Find the x- and y-intercepts for each equation.

1. $y = -2x + 8$

x-intercept: _____

y-intercept: _____

2. $\frac{1}{2}x + y = -2$

x-intercept: _____

y-intercept: _____

3. $5x - 3y = 11$

x-intercept: _____

y-intercept: _____

Directions Graph each system of equations and identify the point of intersection.

4. $3x - y = -7$

$5x + 5y = -5$

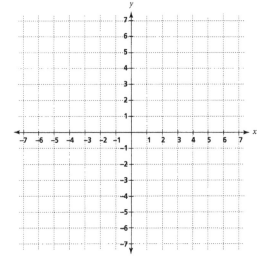

5. $x + y = 2$

$x - y = 4$

And Statements—Conjunctions

EXAMPLE	Study the patterns in the following conjunctions.

$10^1 = 10$ and $10^2 = 100$

T   **T**   **= True**

$3^2 \cdot 3^3 = 3^5$ and $\frac{1}{2} \cdot \frac{2}{1} = \frac{1}{4}$

T   **F**   **= False**

$\sqrt{100} = 50$ and $(-5)^2 = -25$

F   **F**   **= False**

Directions Complete each conjunction in the chart by choosing an appropriate statement from the Statement Box and writing it on the blank. (Hint: In the box, left-side statements are true, right-side are false.)

p	q	$p \wedge q$
$4^3 = 64$	**1.** _____	T
$(3)(9) = 27$	**2.** _____	F
3. _____	$x = 3$ is a vertical line	F
x has a value of 3 in $3x = 9$	**4.** _____	T

Statement Box

$4^2 = 16$	17 is not a prime number
$\frac{1}{2}(14) = 14 \div 2$	$\sqrt{-16} = -4$
$(x^2)(x^3) = x^5$	$a^4 \div a = a^4$
$\sqrt{16} = \pm 4$	$-8 + 8 = -16$

Directions Write your own conjunction so that the value of $p \wedge q$ will be true.

5. _____

Problem Solving Using Linear Equations

EXAMPLE

Dean's cat is one year less than twice the age of Drina's cat. The difference in the cats' ages is 7 years. Find the ages of the two cats.

Step 1 Let x = age of Dean's cat y = age of Drina's cat

$x = 2y - 1$ one less than twice the age

$x - y = 7$ difference in the cats' ages

$x = y + 7$ last equation rewritten to put x on left

Step 2 Solve by substituting $y + 7$ for x in the first equation.

$y = 8$ age of Drina's cat $x = 15$ age of Dean's cat

Step 3 Check by substituting x and y values in both equations.

$x = 2y - 1$ $x - y = 7$

$15 = 2(8) - 1$ $15 - 8 = 7$

$15 = 15$ True $7 = 7$ True

Directions   Use any method to solve each system of equations. Check your answer.

1. $x + y = 9$

$x - 2y = -6$

2. $x + y = 14$

$x - y = 10$

3. $2x + 3y = 2$

$8x - 3y = 3$

Directions   Use systems of equations to solve the problems.

4. A farmer raises wheat and oats on 180 acres. She plants wheat on 20 more acres than she plants oats on. How many acres of each crop does the farmer plant?

5. Enrico says, "I'm thinking of 2 mystery numbers. One number is 3 times the other. The sum of the two numbers is 48." What are Enrico's mystery numbers?

Introduction to Matrices: Addition and Subtraction

EXAMPLE   Add the matrices.

$$\begin{bmatrix} 1 & 4 \\ 6 & 5 \end{bmatrix} + \begin{bmatrix} 6 & 5 \\ 3 & 5 \end{bmatrix}$$

Step 1   Add corresponding entries or members of each matrix.

$$\begin{bmatrix} 1+6 & 4+5 \\ 6+3 & 5+5 \end{bmatrix}$$

Step 2   Write the sums in matrix form.

$$\begin{bmatrix} 7 & 9 \\ 9 & 10 \end{bmatrix}$$

Subtract the matrices.

$$\begin{bmatrix} 10 & 87 & 21 \\ -6 & 12 & 7 \end{bmatrix} - \begin{bmatrix} 7 & 88 & 0 \\ -8 & 12 & 6 \end{bmatrix}$$

Step 1   Subtract corresponding entries or members of each matrix.

$$\begin{bmatrix} 10-7 & 87-88 & 21-0 \\ (-6)-(8) & 12-12 & 7-6 \end{bmatrix}$$

Step 2   Write the differences in matrix form.

$$\begin{bmatrix} 3 & -1 & 21 \\ 2 & 0 & 1 \end{bmatrix}$$

Directions   Add or subtract the matrices.

1. $\begin{bmatrix} 5 & 9 \\ -8 & 6 \end{bmatrix} + \begin{bmatrix} 7 & 14 \\ 12 & 94 \end{bmatrix}$

2. $\begin{bmatrix} 8 & 4 \\ 6 & 5 \\ 12 & 21 \end{bmatrix} + \begin{bmatrix} 6 & 47 \\ 4 & 34 \\ 72 & 5 \end{bmatrix}$

3. $\begin{bmatrix} 33 & 41 & 36 & 59 \\ 76 & 15 & 87 & 5 \\ 21 & 32 & 43 & 54 \\ -8 & -14 & -51 & -23 \end{bmatrix} + \begin{bmatrix} 8 & 6 & 12 & 7 \\ -6 & -12 & -98 & -5 \\ 54 & 43 & 32 & 21 \\ -9 & 0 & -35 & -77 \end{bmatrix}$

4. $\begin{bmatrix} 52 & 36 \\ -9 & 93 \end{bmatrix} - \begin{bmatrix} 27 & 27 \\ 14 & 94 \end{bmatrix}$

5. $\begin{bmatrix} 61 & 23 & 17 \\ -16 & 31 & 7 \end{bmatrix} - \begin{bmatrix} 13 & 47 & 17 \\ -28 & 0 & 36 \end{bmatrix}$

Multiplication of Matrices

EXAMPLE Let $A = \begin{bmatrix} 2 & 3 \\ 5 & 1 \end{bmatrix}$.　　　　Find 4A.

Multiply each entry by 4.　　$\begin{bmatrix} 4 \cdot 2 & 4 \cdot 3 \\ 4 \cdot 5 & 4 \cdot 1 \end{bmatrix}$　$4A = \begin{bmatrix} 8 & 12 \\ 20 & 4 \end{bmatrix}$

EXAMPLE Let $X = \begin{bmatrix} 4 & 6 \\ 5 & 7 \end{bmatrix}$.　　Let $Y = \begin{bmatrix} 8 & 9 \\ 2 & 3 \end{bmatrix}$.

Multiply matrix X by matrix Y.　$\begin{bmatrix} 4 & 6 \\ 5 & 7 \end{bmatrix} \times \begin{bmatrix} 8 & 9 \\ 2 & 3 \end{bmatrix}$

Step 1 Multiply the rows in X by the columns in Y.　　**Step 2** Add the products.

$\begin{bmatrix} 4 \bullet 8 + 6 \bullet 2 & 4 \bullet 9 + 6 \bullet 3 \\ 5 \bullet 8 + 7 \bullet 2 & 5 \bullet 9 + 7 \bullet 3 \end{bmatrix}$　　　　　$\begin{bmatrix} 32 + 12 & 36 + 18 \\ 40 + 14 & 45 + 21 \end{bmatrix}$

$X \times Y = \begin{bmatrix} 44 & 54 \\ 54 & 66 \end{bmatrix}$

Directions Find the product of each matrix and the number shown.

1. $3 \times \begin{bmatrix} 3 & 8 \\ 9 & 5 \end{bmatrix}$　　　　　　　**2.** $7 \times \begin{bmatrix} 10 & 15 & 20 \\ 6 & 8 & 10 \\ 4 & 2 & 0 \end{bmatrix}$

3. $y \times \begin{bmatrix} x & 4 & 17 \\ 2x & 9 & 0 \\ 3x & 1 & y \end{bmatrix}$

Directions Multiply the two matrices.

4. $\begin{bmatrix} x & y \\ n & r \end{bmatrix} \times \begin{bmatrix} 4 & 5 \\ 6 & 7 \end{bmatrix}$　　　　　**5.** $\begin{bmatrix} 9 & 10 & 11 \\ 14 & 15 & 16 \end{bmatrix} \times \begin{bmatrix} 8 & 4 \\ -1 & \frac{1}{2} \\ 14 & 0 \end{bmatrix}$

Rational Numbers as Decimals

EXAMPLE   Is the decimal form of these fractions *terminating* or *repeating*? $\frac{1}{5}$ $\frac{2}{3}$

     Step 1   Divide numerator by denominator.

$$5\overline{)1.000} \quad \begin{array}{r} .2000 \\ \hline \end{array}$$
$$\begin{array}{r} \underline{10} \\ 0 \end{array}$$

            Divide numerator by denominator.

$$3\overline{)2.000000} \quad \begin{array}{r} .666 \ldots \\ \hline \end{array}$$
$$\begin{array}{r} \underline{18} \\ 20 \\ \underline{18} \\ 20 \ldots \end{array}$$

     Step 2 $\frac{1}{5} = 0.2\overline{0}$ Terminating $\frac{2}{3} = 0.\overline{6}$ Repeating

---

Directions   Write the decimal expansion for these rational numbers. Tell whether each is *terminating* or *repeating*.

1. $\frac{1}{4}$ _____   **6.** $\frac{1}{9}$ _____

2. $\frac{4}{5}$ _____   **7.** $\frac{7}{8}$ _____

3. $\frac{19}{20}$ _____   **8.** $\frac{11}{25}$ _____

4. $\frac{5}{6}$ _____   **9.** $\frac{1}{5}$ _____

5. $\frac{2}{15}$ _____   **10.** $\frac{2}{7}$ _____

Directions   Using a calculator, perform the division to change each fraction into an expanded decimal. Tell whether each is *terminating* or *repeating*.

11. $\frac{1}{11}$ _____   **16.** $\frac{1}{13}$ _____

12. $\frac{8}{9}$ _____   **17.** $\frac{7}{10}$ _____

13. $\frac{3}{8}$ _____   **18.** $\frac{13}{15}$ _____

14. $\frac{1}{16}$ _____   **19.** $\frac{6}{7}$ _____

15. $\frac{3}{4}$ _____   **20.** $\frac{69}{80}$ _____

Rational Number Equivalents

EXAMPLE   What rational number is equal to $0.58\overline{3}$?

Step 1 Let $x = 0.58333...$

Step 2 Multiply to place the first repeating digit(s) to the *left* of the decimal.

$(1000)x = (1000)0.583333...$ Simplify: $1000x = 583.333...$

Step 3 Multiply to place the repeating digit(s) to the *right* of the decimal.

$(100)x = (100)0.583333...$ Simplify: $100x = 58.333...$

Step 4 Subtract the smaller from the larger result.

$1000x = 583.333...$

$$\frac{-100x = 58.333...}{900x = 525.000}$$

$x = \frac{525}{900}$ Simplify: $\frac{525}{900} \div \frac{75}{75} = \frac{7}{12}$

Directions Find the rational number equivalents for these decimal expansions. Show your work.

1. $0.1\overline{3}$ _____

2. $0.8\overline{3}$ _____

3. $0.\overline{1}$ _____

4. $0.\overline{6}$ _____

5. $0.8\overline{6}$ _____

6. $0.\overline{8}$ _____

7. $0.1\overline{6}$ _____

8. $0.\overline{36}$ _____

9. $0.\overline{18}$ _____

10. $0.\overline{4}$ _____

Irrational Numbers as Decimals

EXAMPLE   Find each root. Tell whether it is *rational* or *irrational*.

$\sqrt{3}$ $\sqrt[3]{27}$

Using a calculator: $\sqrt{3} = 1.73205...$ Using a calculator: $\sqrt[3]{27} = 3.0$

The number is *irrational* because it neither ends in zeroes nor has a repeating pattern.   The number is *rational* because it ends in zeroes.

Directions   Complete the chart. Find each root and tell whether it is *rational* or *irrational*. You may use a calculator.

Radical	Root	Rational or Irrational?
$\sqrt{49}$	1. _____	2. _____
$\sqrt{15}$	3. _____	4. _____
$\sqrt{11}$	5. _____	6. _____
$\sqrt{6}$	7. _____	8. _____
$\sqrt{144}$	9. _____	10. _____
$\sqrt{121}$	11. _____	12. _____
$\sqrt{50}$	13. _____	14. _____
$\sqrt[3]{50}$	15. _____	16. _____
$\sqrt{36}$	17. _____	18. _____
$\sqrt[3]{18}$	19. _____	20. _____
$\sqrt{169}$	21. _____	22. _____
$\sqrt[3]{125}$	23. _____	24. _____

Directions   Solve the problem.

25. Caitlin has cut out a square piece of graph paper that contains a total of 81 blocks. How many blocks are there along one side of the square?

_____

Products and Quotients of Radicals

EXAMPLE

Simplify $\sqrt{48}$.

$$\sqrt{48} = \sqrt{16 \cdot 3} = \sqrt{16} \cdot \sqrt{3} = 4\sqrt{3}$$

Simplify $\sqrt{27x^3}$.

$$\sqrt{27x^3} = \sqrt{27} \cdot \sqrt{x^3} = (\sqrt{9} \cdot \sqrt{3})(\sqrt{x^2} \cdot \sqrt{x}) = (3\sqrt{3})(x\sqrt{x}) = 3x\sqrt{3x}$$

Check. $(3x\sqrt{3x})^2 = 9x^2 \cdot 3x = 27x^3$ True

Directions Simplify the following radicals. Check your answers.

1. $\sqrt{12}$ _____

2. $\sqrt{20}$ _____

3. $\sqrt{48}$ _____

4. $\sqrt{18}$ _____

5. $\sqrt{32}$ _____

6. $\sqrt{50}$ _____

7. $\sqrt{84}$ _____

8. $\sqrt{180a^2b^3}$ _____

9. $\sqrt{98}$ _____

10. $\sqrt{45}$ _____

11. $\sqrt{16xy^2}$ _____

12. $\sqrt{96}$ _____

13. $\sqrt{3a^2}$ _____

14. $\sqrt{45x^2y^3}$ _____

15. $\sqrt{8x^3y^3}$ _____

16. $\sqrt{25x^2y^3}$ _____

17. $\sqrt{1,000}$ _____

18. $\sqrt{396x^2}$ _____

19. $\sqrt{9x^2y}$ _____

20. $\sqrt{32k^3}$ _____

21. $\sqrt{12a^7b^7}$ _____

22. $\sqrt{18x^3y^5}$ _____

23. $\sqrt{50a^3b^5}$ _____

24. $\sqrt{192}$ _____

Directions Solve the problem.

25. To repair a wall, Van and Mai have cut out a square piece of wallboard whose area is 396 square inches. The length of one side of this piece is $\sqrt{396}$ inches. Use the first rule of radicals to simplify this expression.

_____

Sums and Differences of Radicals

EXAMPLE   Find the sum of $\sqrt{2} + \sqrt{18}$.

   Step 1 Simplify $\sqrt{18}$. $\sqrt{18} = \sqrt{(9 \cdot 2)} = \sqrt{9} \cdot \sqrt{2} = 3\sqrt{2}$

   Step 2 Add. $\sqrt{2} + 3\sqrt{2} = (1)\sqrt{2} + 3\sqrt{2} = (1 + 3)\sqrt{2} = 4\sqrt{2}$

   Subtract $\sqrt{12} - \sqrt{3}$.

   Step 1 Simplify. $\sqrt{12} = \sqrt{(4 \cdot 3)} = \sqrt{4} \cdot \sqrt{3} = 2\sqrt{3}$

   Step 2 Subtract. $2\sqrt{3} - (1)\sqrt{3} = (1)\sqrt{3} = \sqrt{3}$

Directions Add or subtract. If you cannot add or subtract, write
not possible.

1. $3\sqrt{2} + 5\sqrt{2}$ _____

2. $\sqrt{20} + \sqrt{45}$ _____

3. $3\sqrt{2} + 5\sqrt{7}$ _____

4. $\sqrt{18} - \sqrt{8}$ _____

5 $\sqrt{21} + 3\sqrt{21}$ _____

6. $9\sqrt{2} - \sqrt{18}$ _____

7. $\sqrt{12} + \sqrt{27}$ _____

8. $6\sqrt{14} - 2\sqrt{7}$ _____

9. $\sqrt{72} - \sqrt{32}$ _____

10. $\sqrt{20} + \sqrt{180}$ _____

11. $3\sqrt{2} + 5\sqrt{8}$ _____

12. $\sqrt{12} - \sqrt{48}$ _____

13. $\sqrt{2x^2} + \sqrt{8x^2}$ _____

14. $\sqrt{24} + 2\sqrt{54}$ _____

15. $\sqrt{8x^2y} + \sqrt{18x^2y}$ _____

16. $2\sqrt{12} - \sqrt{5}$ _____

17. $8\sqrt{96} - 5\sqrt{24}$ _____

18. $3\sqrt{125} - 2\sqrt{80}$ _____

19. $\sqrt{1,000} - \sqrt{360}$ _____

20. $\sqrt{6x^2} - x\sqrt{54}$ _____

Radicals and Fractions

EXAMPLE Rationalize the denominator of $\frac{3}{4\sqrt{2}}$.

$$\frac{3}{4\sqrt{2}} \cdot \frac{\sqrt{2}}{\sqrt{2}} = \frac{3\sqrt{2}}{4 \cdot 2} = \frac{3\sqrt{2}}{8}$$

Directions Rationalize the denominator of each fraction. Be sure your answer is in simplest form.

1. $\frac{3}{\sqrt{3}}$ _____

2. $\frac{1}{\sqrt{2}}$ _____

3. $\frac{5}{\sqrt{5}}$ _____

4. $\frac{5}{\sqrt{20}}$ _____

5. $\frac{1}{\sqrt{7}}$ _____

6. $\frac{4}{\sqrt{12}}$ _____

7. $\frac{1}{\sqrt{5}}$ _____

8. $\frac{10}{\sqrt{x}}$ _____

9. $\frac{9}{\sqrt{27}}$ _____

10. $\frac{\sqrt{9}}{\sqrt{2x}}$ _____

EXAMPLE Rationalize the denominator of $\frac{1}{2-\sqrt{2}}$.

The conjugate of $2 - \sqrt{2}$ is $2 + \sqrt{2}$.

$$\frac{1}{2-\sqrt{2}} \cdot \frac{2+\sqrt{2}}{2+\sqrt{2}} = \frac{2+\sqrt{2}}{4-2} = \frac{2+\sqrt{2}}{2}$$

You cannot further simplify, because the 2 in the numerator is a separate term.

Directions Use a conjugate to rationalize the denominator of each fraction. Be sure your answer is in simplest form.

11. $\frac{2}{\sqrt{3}-1}$ _____

12. $\frac{2}{3-\sqrt{2}}$ _____

13. $\frac{3}{\sqrt{3}-1}$ _____

14. $\frac{2}{2-\sqrt{2}}$ _____

15. $\frac{12}{3-\sqrt{3}}$ _____

Radicals in Equations

EXAMPLE Solve for x: $\sqrt{x} + 2 = 13$

 Step 1 Isolate the variable, x. $\sqrt{x} + 2 - 2 = 13 - 2$

$\sqrt{x} = 11$

 Step 2 Square both sides. $(\sqrt{x})^2 = 11^2$

$x = 121$

 Step 3 Check. $\sqrt{121} + 2 = 13$

$11 + 2 = 13 \qquad 13 = 13$

True

Directions Solve each equation for the variable. Check your answers.

1. $\sqrt{x} = 5$ _____

2. $\sqrt{n} = 8$ _____

3. $\sqrt{k + 3} = 2$ _____

4. $\sqrt{a} = 13$ _____

5. $\sqrt{r + 8} = 12$ _____

6. $\sqrt{y - 5} = 5$ _____

7. $\sqrt{m} = 16$ _____

8. $\sqrt{4n - 3} = 3$ _____

Directions Solve the problems. Show the equation as well as your answer.

9. Kristen challenges you with this puzzle: "Add the square root of a mystery number to the square root of 100. The result is 19. What is the mystery number?"

_____

10. Jaime buys a square tablecloth. The package label declares, "The area of this tablecloth is 800 square inches." What is the length of a side of the cloth? (Express your answer as a simplified radical.)

_____

Algebra

Simplifying Equations with Radicals

EXAMPLE One way to simplify an equation containing a radical sign is to raise each side of the equation to the second power.

Suppose an object is dropped from a tall building. At the moment the object reaches a velocity of 24 feet per second, how far has the object fallen? Use the formula $V = \sqrt{64d}$ where V = velocity in feet per second and d = distance in feet.

Solution: $V = \sqrt{64d}$

$24 = \sqrt{64d}$

$(24)^2 = (\sqrt{64d}\,)^2$

$576 = 64d$

$9 = d$ The object has fallen 9 feet.

Directions Use a calculator to solve these problems.

1. Suppose the formula $V = \sqrt{32d}$ is used to find the distance in feet (d) an object falls at a velocity (V) measured in feet per second. An object is dropped from the edge of a roof. At the moment the object reaches a velocity of 36 feet per second, it hits the ground. How far did the object fall? _____

2. Suppose the formula $S = 5.5\sqrt{d}$ is used to determine the distance in feet (d) it takes an automobile to stop if it were traveling a certain speed in miles per hour (S). Find the distance it would take an automobile traveling 70 miles per hour to stop. Round your answer to the nearest whole number. _____

3. Suppose the formula $d = 0.25\sqrt{h}$ is used to determine the height in inches (h) that a submarine periscope must be for an observer looking through that periscope to see an object that is a distance of (d) miles away. How far does a submarine periscope have to extend above the water to see a surface ship that is 1 mile away? _____

4. A rectangle measures 4 inches by 6 inches. What is the length in inches, to the nearest tenth, of a diagonal of that rectangle? Use the formula $a^2 + b^2 = c^2$, where a and b represent the legs of a right triangle and c represents the hypotenuse. _____

5. A 16-foot ladder is leaning against the side of a building. If the bottom of the ladder is 8 feet from the side of the building, how far above the ground does the ladder touch the building? Use the formula $a^2 + b^2 = c^2$, where a and b represent the legs of a right triangle and c represents the hypotenuse, and round your answer to the nearest tenth. _____

◼▶ **Algebra**

Radicals and Exponents

EXAMPLE   Rewrite $\sqrt[3]{3a}$ using exponents.

$$\sqrt[3]{3a} = 3^{\frac{1}{3}} \cdot a^{\frac{1}{3}}$$

Directions Rewrite each expression using exponents.

1. $\sqrt[3]{5x}$ _____

2. $\sqrt{7b}$ _____

3. $\sqrt[4]{13d}$ _____

4. $\sqrt[3]{5y}$ _____

5. $\sqrt{17xy}$ _____

6. $\sqrt[7]{11ab}$ _____

EXAMPLE   Write $w \cdot \sqrt[3]{w}$ with exponents and simplify.

$$w \cdot \sqrt[3]{w} = w^1 \cdot w^{\frac{1}{3}} = w^{(1 + \frac{1}{3})} = w^{\frac{4}{3}}$$

Directions Simplify using exponents. Then find the products.

7. $c \cdot \sqrt{c}$ _____

8. $n \cdot \sqrt[3]{n}$ _____

9. $d^2 \cdot \sqrt[3]{d}$ _____

10. $x^3 \cdot \sqrt{x}$ _____

11. $y^2 \cdot \sqrt[6]{y}$ _____

12. $b^3 \cdot \sqrt[7]{b}$ _____

EXAMPLE   Simplify $\sqrt{3^3}$.

$$\sqrt{3^3} = (3^3)^{\frac{1}{2}} = 3^{\frac{3}{2}}$$

Directions Rewrite each expression using exponents. Then find the product.

13. $\sqrt[3]{a^2}$ _____

14. $\sqrt[3]{k^5}$ _____

15. $\sqrt[5]{n^2}$ _____

16. $\sqrt[7]{m^3}$ _____

17. $\sqrt[5]{c^3}$ _____

18. $\sqrt[4]{b^5}$ _____

19. $\sqrt{x^5}$ _____

20. $\sqrt[3]{n^4}$ _____

Drawing and Using a Square Root Graph

EXAMPLE

Use the square root graph to find the value of x when $x^2 = 20$.

Step 1 Find $y = 20$ on the y-axis. Follow the dashed horizontal line to the square root graph (curved solid line). The point at which the dashed line meets the graph is $(x, 20)$, where $20 = x^2$.

Step 2 Follow the dashed vertical line from $(x, 20)$ to the x-axis. The dashed line intersects the x-axis at the value, $x = \sqrt{20}$.

Step 3 Read the approximate value: $x \approx 4.5$.

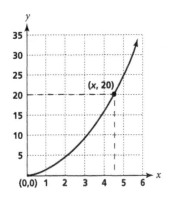

Directions Use the square root graph to find the following square roots. Estimate to the nearest tenth.

1. $\sqrt{2}$ _____

2. $\sqrt{30}$ _____

3. $\sqrt{10}$ _____

4. $\sqrt{27}$ _____

5. $\sqrt{12}$ _____

6. $\sqrt{23}$ _____

7. $\sqrt{14}$ _____

8. $\sqrt{8}$ _____

9. $\sqrt{17}$ _____

10 $\sqrt{28}$ _____

Angles and Angle Measure

EXAMPLE   Identify angle pairs.

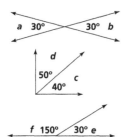

∠a and ∠b are *vertical* angles.

∠c and ∠d are *complementary* angles.

∠e and ∠f are *supplementary* angles.

Directions   Describe each pair of angles. Use one of the following words:
vertical, complementary, supplementary.

Diagram 1   **Diagram 2**   **Diagram 3**   **Diagram 4**

      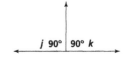

1. ∠g, ∠h   _____   **3.** ∠r, ∠s   _____

2. ∠p, ∠q   _____   **4.** ∠j, ∠k   _____

EXAMPLE   Study these angles. The letter *m* stands for *measure of.*

Acute angle   Right angle   Obtuse angle

0° < m < 90°   m = 90°   90° < m < 180°

Directions   Refer to diagrams 1–4 on this page and answer the questions.

5. Is ∠g acute?   _____   **8.** Is ∠j a right angle?   _____

6. Is ∠r a right angle?   _____   **9.** Is ∠k acute?   _____

7. Is ∠h obtuse?   _____   **10.** Is ∠s acute?   _____

Pairs of Lines in a Plane and in Space

EXAMPLE Intersecting lines, *m* and *n*

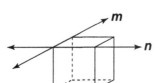

Parallel lines, *m* and *n*

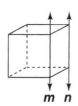

Skew lines, *m* and *n*

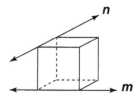

Directions Identify lines *r* and *s* in each figure. Write *intersecting*, *parallel*, or *skew*.

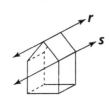

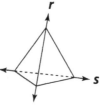

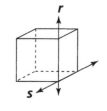

1. _____

2. _____

3. _____

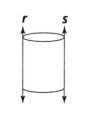

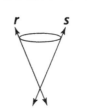

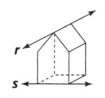

4. _____

5. _____

6. _____

EXAMPLE A transversal, *t*, intersects two or more lines.

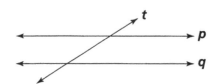

Directions If *t* is a transversal, write *yes*. Otherwise, write *no*.

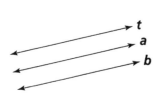

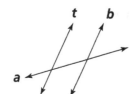

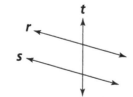

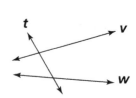

7. _____

8. _____

9. _____

10. _____

Angle Measures in a Triangle

EXAMPLE

Theorem

m∠A + m∠B + m∠C = 180°

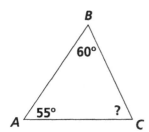

Find the measure of ∠C.

Let n = m∠C.

n + 60° + 55° = 180°   Solve: n = 65°

Theorem

m∠A + m∠B = m∠y

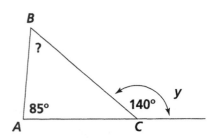

Find the measure of ∠B.

Let k = m∠B.

85° + k = 140°   Solve: k = 55°

Directions Find m∠x in each triangle.

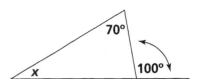

1. _____   **2.** _____   **3.** _____

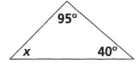

4. _____   **5.** _____

Algebra

Naming Triangles

EXAMPLE Triangles can be classified according to their sides.

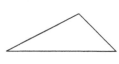

Scalene   **Isosceles**   **Equilateral**

Directions Fill in the chart by writing the classification word to describe the triangle with the given sides.

Triangle—Measurements of the Sides	Classification
2.5 inches, 1.5 inches, 2.0 inches	1. _____
11 cm, 8 cm, 6.5 cm	2. _____
2 feet, 3 feet, 3 feet	3. _____
35 mm, 35 mm, 35 mm	4. _____
5 units, 10 units, 5 units	5. _____

EXAMPLE Triangles can be classified according to their angles.

Acute   **Equiangular**   **Obtuse**   **Right**

Directions Fill in the chart by writing the classification word to describe the triangle with the given angles.

Triangle—Measurements of the Angles	Classification
60°, 60°, 60°	6. _____
30°, 110°, 40°	7. _____
60°, 15°, 105°	8. _____
90°, 70°, 20°	9. _____
70°, 30°, 80°	10. _____

Quadrilaterals

EXAMPLE   Find m∠D in the parallelogram.

Step 1 Because $\overline{AB} \parallel \overline{CD}$, ∠A and ∠D are supplementary. Thus, 50° + m∠D = 180°.

Step 2 Solve for m∠D.

50° + m∠D = 180°

50° + m∠D − 50° = 180° − 50°

m∠D = 130°

Step 3 Check.   50° + m∠D = 180°   50° + 130°= 180°   True

Directions Find the measures of the angles in the isosceles trapezoid.

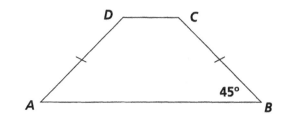

1. ∠A _____   **2.** ∠C _____   **3.** ∠D _____

Directions Tell whether enough information is given to calculate the measures of the angles in each described figure. Explain your answer.

4. Given: The figure is a rectangle.

_____

_____

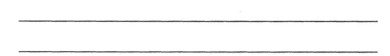

5. Given: The figure is a trapezoid in which no sides are equal.

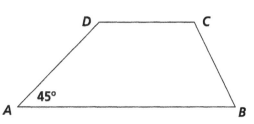

_____

_____

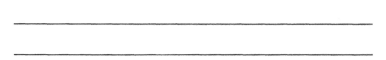

Congruent and Similar Triangles

EXAMPLE   Are these triangles congruent? Give a reason for the answer.

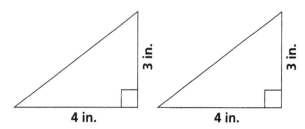

Yes. They are congruent by the Side-Angle-Side (SAS) theorem, which states that if two sides and the included angle of two triangles are equal, the triangles are congruent.

Directions Tell whether each pair of triangles is congruent. If the pair is congruent, name the theorem that proves congruence (SAS, SSS, ASA).

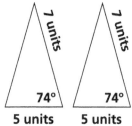

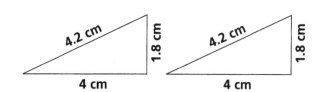

1. _____ _____   **2.** _____ _____

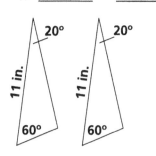

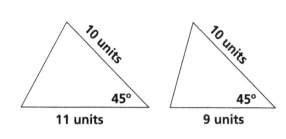

3. _____ _____   **4.** _____ _____

Directions Answer the question.

5. Are all right triangles similar? Tell why or why not.

_____

_____

Trigonometric Ratios

EXAMPLE

Find the value of *x*, using trigonometric (trig) ratios.

Step 1 Set up an equation using the appropriate trig ratio. Since the side opposite from the given angle and the hypotenuse are known, use the sine (or sin) ratio.

$\sin 50° = \frac{x}{9}$

Step 2 Using a calculator, find and substitute the sine value.

$0.766 = \frac{x}{9}$

Step 3 Solve for *x*.

x = 6.894 or approximately 6.9 units.

Directions Find the value of *x* to the nearest tenth. Use a calculator.

1. _____

2. _____

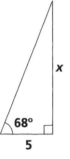

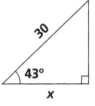

3. _____

4. _____

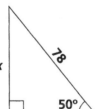

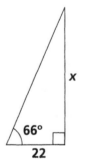

Directions Solve the problem.

5. On a summer afternoon, a smokestack casts an 8-meter shadow. At this time of day, rays from the sun are striking the ground at an angle of 75°. To the nearest tenth of a meter, how high is the smokestack?

_____

Solutions by Factoring

EXAMPLE

Put $6x^2 = x + 15$ in standard quadratic form.

Step 1 Match the terms with terms in the standard form.

Standard Quadratic Form: $ax^2 + bx + c = 0$

$6x^2 = (1)x + 15$

Step 2 Subtract x from both sides of the equation.

$6x^2 - x = x + 15 - x$ Result: $6x^2 - x = 15$

Step 3 Subtract 15 from both sides of the equation.

$6x^2 - x - 15 = 15 - 15$ Result: $6x^2 - x - 15 = 0$

Directions Rearrange the terms of each equation to put it in standard quadratic form: $ax^2 + bx + c = 0$.

1. $x^2 = -6 - 5x$ _____

2. $2x + 15 = x^2$ _____

3. $y^2 - 7y + 6 = -4$ _____

4. $3x = 2 - 2x^2$ _____

EXAMPLE

Solve $x^2 - 3x - 4 = 0$ by factoring.

Step 1 Factor: $(x - 4)(x + 1) = 0$

Step 2 Set each factor = 0, and solve for x.

$x - 4 = 0$ $x + 1 = 0$

    $x = 4$ $x = -1$

Step 3 Check the results.

$(4)^2 - 3(4) - 4 = 0$ $(-1)^2 - 3(-1) - 4 = 0$

           $0 = 0$ True $0 = 0$ True

Directions Use factoring to solve the equation you rearranged in problem 1 above.

5. _____

Writing the Equations from Their Roots

EXAMPLE   The roots of a quadratic equation are –1 and –3. What is
the general form of the equation?

Step 1 Given the roots, $x = -1$ or $x = -3$.

Step 2 Set the factors equal to zero. $(x + 1) = 0$ $(x + 3) = 0$

Step 3 Multiply the factors. $(x + 1)(x + 3) = 0$

Step 4 Use the distributive property to place the
equation in general form. $x^2 + 4x + 3 = 0$

Directions Find the quadratic equation that has these roots.

1. –3, 2   _____

2. –1, 4   _____

3. –6, 3   _____

4. 2, 5   _____

5. –6, 1   _____

6. –10, 2   _____

7. 2, 3   _____

8. –5, –2   _____

9. –3, 5   _____

10. 12, 1   _____

11. –8, 2   _____

12. –5, 10   _____

13. –7, 5   _____

14. –5, 6   _____

15. –8, 4   _____

Solving by Completing the Square

EXAMPLE   Find the roots of $x^2 + 4x - 3 = 0$ by completing the square.

Step 1   Rewrite the equation so that the constant is isolated.

$x^2 + 4x = 3$

Step 2   Find the constant that must be added to complete the square.
Take $\frac{1}{2}$ of the x coefficient and square it.

$\frac{1}{2}(4) = 2$ $2^2 = 4$

Step 3   Add the constant to both sides of the equation.

$x^2 + 4x + 4 = 3 + 4$ Result: $x^2 + 4x + 4 = 7$

Step 4   Factor the trinomial on the left side, and solve for x.

$(x + 2)^2 = 7$ Therefore, $x + 2 = \pm \sqrt{7}$

$x = -2 + \sqrt{7}$ or $x = -2 - \sqrt{7}$

Step 5   Check by substituting the roots in the equation.

Directions   Find the roots of each equation by completing the square.

1. $x^2 + 4x + 3 = 0$ _____

2. $x^2 - 2x = 0$ _____

3. $m^2 - 6m - 7 = 0$ _____

4. $k^2 + 12k = 0$ _____

5. $y^2 + 8y - 9 = 0$ _____

6. $x^2 - 10x = 0$ _____

7. $x^2 - 6x + 2 = 0$ _____

8. $a^2 - 4a - 12 = 0$ _____

9. $x^2 - 2x - 15 = 0$ _____

10. $d^2 - 2d - 24 = 0$ _____

Solving Using the Quadratic Formula

EXAMPLE

Use the quadratic formula to find roots of $x^2 + 5x + 6 = 0$.

$$x = \frac{-b \pm \sqrt{b^2 - 4ac}}{2a}$$

Values of a, b, and c from the equation: $\quad a = 1 \quad b = 5 \quad c = 6$

Substitute: $\quad x = \frac{-5 \pm \sqrt{5^2 - 4(1)(6)}}{2(1)}$

$$x = -2 \text{ or } -3$$

To check, substitute the roots in the original equation.

Directions Use the quadratic formula to find the roots of these equations. Remember to write the equation in standard form first.

1. $y^2 - 5y + 6 = 0$ _____

2. $x^2 + 7x + 12 = 0$ _____

3. $2n^2 - n - 1 = 0$ _____

4. $x^2 = 3x + 4$ _____

EXAMPLE

Check that the roots of the equation are valid.

$2x^2 + 4x - 2 = 0 \qquad$ Roots: $-1 + \sqrt{2}$ or $-1 - \sqrt{2}$

Substitute for x: $\qquad 2(-1 + \sqrt{2})^2 + 4(-1 + \sqrt{2}) - 2 = 0$

$\qquad\qquad 0 = 0 \quad$ Therefore, $-1 + \sqrt{2}$ is valid.

Substitute for x: $\qquad 2(-1 - \sqrt{2})^2 + 4(-1 - \sqrt{2}) - 2 = 0$

$\qquad\qquad 0 = 0 \quad$ Therefore, $-1 - \sqrt{2}$ is valid.

Directions Check the roots of the equation. Tell whether they are valid.

5. $x^2 - 2x - 4 = 0 \qquad$ Roots: $1 + \sqrt{5}$ or $1 - \sqrt{5}$

_____

Graphing Quadratic Equations

EXAMPLE   The graph of a quadratic equation is a parabola.

The graph box shows the parabola graph of $y = x^2 + 4x + 1$.

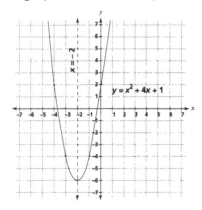

Calculate the *axis of symmetry* for this quadratic graph.

a = coefficient of x^2 = 1 b = coefficient of x = 4

Formula: $x = \frac{-b}{2a}$ Substitute: $\frac{-4}{2(1)} = -2$

The axis of symmetry is $x = -2$. It is the dashed line on the graph.

Directions   Use this equation to answer problems 1–5: $y = x^2 - 3x + 2$.

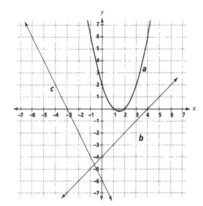

1. Identify the graph of the equation. Write its letter here.   _____

2. Find the point $(2, 0)$. Is it on the graph of the equation?   _____

3. Find the point $(-2, 3)$. Is it on the graph of the equation?   _____

4. Use $x = \frac{-b}{2a}$ to calculate the axis of symmetry.   _____

5. Plot the axis of symmetry on the graph.
